The Organic Money Making Kit 2-in-1 value Bundle:

Great profit making ideas to sustainably start your own business from home & How to make money in high school and college

from various sources. Please consult a licensed professional before attempting any techniques outlined in this book.

By reading this document, the reader agrees that under no circumstances is the author responsible for any losses, direct or indirect, that are incurred as a result of the use of the information contained within this document, including, but not limited to, errors, omissions, or inaccuracies.

Table of Contents

Home-Based Jobs & Sustainable Crafts

Introduction 10

Chapter 1: The Secret to Understanding
How the Pricing System Works 16

    Supply and Demand 16

    Market Forces 18

    Elasticity and Government Policy 20

    Efficiency of Markets.................................... 21

    Firms in Competitive Markets 22

    Monopolies and Oligopolies.......................26

Chapter 2: Discover the Economic Concepts
Everyone Uses, but No One Talks About.........30

    Microeconomics 32

    Macroeconomics...39

Chapter 3: Proven Principles of Economics
to Be Successful and Outsmart 99% of the
population 44

Chapter 4: The Future of Entrepreneurship....56

    How Can You Use These Principles to
    Become Successful?......................................56

Chapter 5: Applying Economic Principles to
Today's World 70

    Digital Entrepreneurship 72

A Short message from the Author: 84

Chapter 6: The Secret to Earning Income
with Recycled and Upcycled Materials 85

Chapter 7: The Complete Guide to
Producing Your Own Food for Profit............. 102
Chapter 8: The Ultimate Slow Fashion
Guide for Anyone 118
Chapter 9: Selling Used Books...................... 132
Chapter 10: Candle Making 145
Conclusion..161
References 166

How to Make Money in High School and College

Introduction 180
   Some Cold, Hard Facts 181
   How This Book Will Help You 186
   Who Am I? 188
Chapter 1: Neighborhood Jobs 190
   Neighborhood Jobs 191
Chapter 2: Offer Your Skills 224
   Money Making Ideas 225
Chapter 3: Be Employed 249
   Employment Opportunities 249
Chapter 4: Create Something to Sell 265
   Making Useful Items 265
Chapter 5: Trade Anything 282
   Start Trading With These Methods 282
Chapter 6: Earn from Ads 297
   Creating Content to Attract Advertisers 297
Chapter 7: Getting into the Nitty Gritty of Making Money 313
   Administrative Responsibilities 313
   Taxes 318
Chapter 8: What to Do With Your Money 321
   Saving Money 322
   Investing Your Money 327
Conclusion 330
Join our inner circle 334
References 335

Home-Based Jobs & Sustainable Crafts

Key Knowledge You Need to Acquire Now to Understand Basic Economics, Make Organic Money, and Profit in Today's Hotter World

Clement Harrison

Do **NOT** continue reading before you watch <u>this 7-minute video</u>... or you will regret it!

Discover the <u>ESSENTIAL CONCEPTS OF ECONOMICS</u> that everyone needs to know within 7-minutes

SCAN ME

This 7-minute video will give you a powerful edge over everyone else by:

- Discovering how to <u>leverage economic tools</u>
- Making you <u>understand our spending habits</u>
- <u>Predicting</u> economic <u>human behavior</u>
- <u>Understanding the markets</u> and the macro economy

SCAN ME

>> to access this must-watch video and make sure you obtain a much better understanding of the world around you

Introduction

Entrepreneurship is the word of the month these days and everyone is looking for the pot of gold at the end of the proverbial rainbow. You only need to scroll through the internet to see just how many get-rich-quick schemes and work from home offers there are out there. Ideas and guidelines on how to start a home-based business are peppered throughout social media so often that it is not only becoming hard to miss, but everyone wants a piece of the entrepreneurial pie. While almost all seem legitimate, some just seem too hard to believe, and not all of the information offered can be useful in the long term.

Now, who wouldn't want to make a little money on the side with a small business? It can give you that little bit of extra cash you need to ease your financial burdens. There are several reasons why people consider starting their businesses: freedom, tax breaks, and having a meaningful life being some of them. Businesses are started for very different reasons by very different people. Entrepreneurship is known to be so successful that there is no reason not to start one. If you're thinking about taking that leap into the business world, then do it, it could be life-changing.

How about thinking a little bigger than just some extra cash, how about turning this into a fully-fledged and lucrative business? It all starts with you, your talents and abilities, your time and effort, as well as what your dreams are for your future. The problem that most people have when trying to start a business is that they don't have a clear, well-thought-out plan to sustain it. Financing is not always readily available, and financial jargon can seem impossible to parse, so they give up. You cannot make money without understanding money. This is the key to starting and sustaining a home-based business.

Business-minded people and small business owners are becoming more environmentally conscious, and many of them have started working to ensure that their products are eco-friendly as well. Starting a home-based, environmentally friendly business is the way to go. Eco-friendly start-up businesses can include anything from supplying products to offering services. People are becoming more aware of the negative effects most large companies have on our environment, so you can use this to your advantage by positioning your business as a friend of the earth and thus attracting customers. Your passion and enthusiasm for the environment will be a calling card to like-minded people, so not only will you be taking care of the earth, but you will also be building a strong business from it.

In this book, we will combine your dream of starting a small, environmentally friendly home-based business, with basic economic principles that can be applied to your business. You will discover how to use the economy to your advantage, thereby putting you miles ahead of others. Understanding the economy and how it works will add considerable value to your business, and you will learn how to reap the benefits of financial success. You have to get the foundation of your business right before you can build on it. Your time is your greatest resource, and investing your time into building a strong foundation by understanding the fundamental principles that drive the market will be the key to your success.

My name is Clement Harrison. I am a professor of Neuroeconomics and a personal development coach. Numerous people from all walks of life read my material to discover how to use psychology and systematic methods to unlock the door to business and personal success. That could mean finding a job you love, earning more money, starting your business or mastering the intricacies of your mind. Even though teaching brings me great joy and students have appreciated the way I have taught them, my greatest passion in life is to see them use what they've learned to become successful in their own lives. This has inspired me to start my very own management consulting firm. My passion has always been to help people become successful by teaching them how to use psychology and systematic methods to their benefit. Anyone can improve their life by becoming someone who can make a difference in today's world.

By the time you come to the end of this book, you will have a greater understanding of how the world works and how the economy functions within it. This knowledge will give you a head start in starting your own business and creating your own wealth. Apply the principles found in this book to your business to make it sustainable and profitable. Help heal the planet and generate a steady stream of income for yourself.

I have received testimonies and words of gratitude from many people saying that these economic principles have helped them not only to look at money differently but to use what they've learned to give them an edge in the business world. They've made subtle changes that have had a great impact on the sustainability of their businesses and in their private lives. I will unveil these same principles to you in this book, principles that are easy to implement and to follow through on.

With my help and knowledge, you will be fully equipped with the skills needed to create or sustain a thriving business. This book will provide support to maintain your time and money while increasing productivity and profits as you build a stable and relevant business. Being able to sustain a business in today's world while ensuring you have a lifetime of wealth is all about discipline and hard work.

Wealth is unlimited and is waiting for someone to reach out and grab it. Time, however, is not. We all have a small window of time given to us, how we use this will determine how successful we become. Sustainable businesses have untapped potential for profit and could result in reversing global warming. Being a responsible business owner in today's world will help you build a strong customer base with those who share the same principles as yourself. There is a huge market for eco-friendly businesses, where you can do your part for the environment without affecting your bottom line.

There is no better time than now to get started. Fulfill your dreams of building a sustainable business and having a lifetime of wealth. You can do all this without leaving a carbon footprint. The economic principles you are about to read are proven facts. The actionable steps identified in this book will yield incredible results for anyone choosing to apply them. Every chapter is packed with knowledge and guidelines that will enhance your business, taking it to the next level. Your perspective on life and the world around you will be changed, allowing you to be more receptive to making sustainability a reality.

Work from home. Make money fast. Save the planet.

Chapter 1:
The Secret to Understanding How the Pricing System Works

Supply and Demand

Supply and demand is a theory used in economics that explains how the supply of and demand for goods and services affects the pricing. When the demand for goods is higher than the supply, the price of said goods goes up, however, when the supply of goods is higher than the demand, the price of the goods goes down. In most cases, if an item's price is far too high, even if there is a demand for it, most consumers will not pay for it. The company then has to lower the price to sell the product. The price of goods also has a significant effect on demand. The higher the price of something, the less demand there is for it. On the other hand, when the product is priced cheaper, the product demand for it will increase.

While this is the general rule of supply and demand, there may be other factors that can influence the cost of products and services. Sometimes cost can be affected by the public's perception of what could happen in the future. For instance, if they think that there will be a shortage of something, this will increase the demand and lead companies to increase their prices. These prices could be inflated by more than 100%.

There are also cases where the supply and demand of certain products do not have an effect on their price or sales in the market. A notable example occurs when companies do not allow you to bring your own food, snacks, or beverages onto their premises, leaving you with no option but to purchase them. This allows the companies to inflate their food and drink prices so much that they are far more expensive than they would be if you bought them elsewhere. These companies can do this because they've created an environment in which there is no competition. Competitive business practices typically serve to correct irregularities in the supply and demand theory. However, there are times when the government may intervene and set a fixed price on goods. Price control can work against the supplier, especially if the price is so low that the demand becomes too high for the supplier to meet, leaving consumers waiting for far too long before the demand is met.

The law of supply and demand affects not only tangible products but also other areas of the economy. Banks are continually adjusting interest rates to increase or decrease the demand for the supply of money. When the interest rates are low, lots more people borrow money, this increases spending and productivity, which lifts the economy. When interest rates are higher, people are dissuaded from spending their money. They tend to save it instead. The Federal Reserve bank has the power to influence the economy by decreasing the interest rates, thus allowing the price of assets to increase and creating employment opportunities. Although the number of assets remains the same during inflation and deflation, the lower rates foster demand for these assets, which increases the cost of the assets. In the same way, high rates decrease the demand for these assets, pushing the price down. Consumers continuously have to adjust the way they spend their money based solely on the decisions of others.

Market Forces

There is a considerable demand for goods or services. The population's demand for things and their availability is not equal. You don't even need to look further than your very own town to see that not everyone's needs are being met. There is only a limited amount of resources available to meet the needs of everyone. The reason that resources are limited is not because there isn't enough to go around. The reason is that we consume far more than we need. This, in turn, leaves those who are not quick or can't afford something with empty hands.

Our society is made up of individuals who are eager to better themselves and individuals who are willing to use someone else's talents to their advantage. This creates a market for one's talents and a willingness to pay for it. For example, if you need a bookcase, but you don't have the skill to make one, you will pay someone who has the ability to build one. This exchange is mutually advantageous and both of you will benefit from this arrangement.

A market is created between individuals who can benefit from each other. Each person is free to choose who he wants to transact with over numerous commodities. He can even choose not to transact at all. It must be understood that economic principles and laws have a significant influence on the market.

Economic theory depends mainly on the feelings and needs of humans. Hunger increases the demand for food; learning increases the demand for books. Human beings are free to choose based on how attractive something appears to them. We tend to choose things that will add value to our lives. Economic theorists study this behavior and then try and predict what will happen in the real world. They try to explain the ripple effect that the change in prices in one market may have on other areas in the market. If a product is in short supply, similar and cheaper versions of this product could be sold at a higher than standard cost.

Elasticity and Government Policy

Price elasticity is a phenomenon that can impact the shifts in a product's supply and demand. Understanding price elasticity will show you how the price of some goods is affected. Certain necessities have a steady price like housing and cars, etc., then there are non-essentials such as eating out that can fluctuate in price. The government uses price elasticity to determine the tax placed on some goods.

Let's take coffee beans as an example. This is the main product of coffee shops. If the government lowers taxes on coffee beans, The coffee shop can choose to decrease the customer's price for coffee depending on the elasticity of demand. A high demand elasticity means that a decrease in the price of coffee causes the demand for coffee to increase at such a high rate that the coffee shop owner can earn more profit at a lower price than the higher price. Benefitting both the coffeeshop owner and the customers

Efficiency of Markets

When money is invested in the stock market, the goal is not only to make more money but also to outperform and beat the market. The amounts reflected in the market are based on all the available information at any given time. Because no one has information that is not yet available, it is unlikely that an investor can predict a return on the stock price. As prices can only reflect the available information, one cannot get more profit than another. Even if you have inside information, you cannot have an edge over another investor. The stock price reflects information ranging from politics to social events, based on the investors' perception of the stock and whether this information is true. Market efficiency, therefore, means that no one can predict market prices. You cannot plan or strategize an investment to beat the market.

There are, however, irregularities that challenge efficiency. There have been investors who beat the market. Warren Buffet, for example, made billions from buying undervalued stock. Now portfolio managers and investment houses have followed suit and some have done well, while others haven't. With so many people profiting and beating the market, is it possible that you can predict the outcome of stocks? Usually, an investor who beats the market does so out of luck and not skill. A market becomes efficient when all the information is accessible and available to the investors at the same time. An investor must then have funds readily available to take advantage of this information.

The availability of information today also allows our everyday market to become effective and adjust prices. There are also laws that protect smaller companies by preventing the more powerful and successful companies from blocking a small company's entry into the market. Usually, the government gets involved and makes the markets more competitive. In some cases, the government's approval is needed before a company can raise its price. The government will examine the company's profit margin before justifying a price change.

Firms in Competitive Markets

Profit is a great motivator in any company. This is the revenue left over after all the company's costs have been paid. It is a monetary reward for shareholders or the owners of the business. Profits can be used to create incentives to cut costs and manufacture new products. Companies that are motivated by profit can spend more money on research and better technology. They become more efficient and innovative. High profit enables the company to pay better wages to their employees. Shareholders provide a source of increased income for a company, so the company needs to pay them generously. This, in turn, will enable the shareholders to release more capital into the business for future financial expansion.

Seeing that a company is under-performing or is not making enough profit to keep the business running discourages shareholders from investing in that company. They usually sell their shares which drives the price of that company's shares down, making it harder to raise funds in the future. Without profit, a company becomes unsustainable and that leads to job loss. Unprofitable firms will have to change or shut their doors. Companies must keep in mind that some products are more profitable during certain times than others. Thus, a percentage of the profit should be saved for unexpected situations, such as recession or a downturn in the economy.

Governments also charge tax on company profits, and this translates into billions each year. High profits are a great reward for entrepreneurs who start a business. If there were no profits in a business, people would be unlikely to set one up. We all need an incentive to motivate us and cash flow to keep the business afloat, and profit can be the key to both. We must, however, pursue profit in a responsible way so that we do not endanger others or cause damage to our environment. Look to start a business that has some longevity and that has steady profits. Quick money ventures can result in reckless risk-taking behavior. Any business's objective is to grow steadily from a small venture to a highly profitable larger company.

Cost of Production - The Role of Profit

There are thousands of businesses that provide a wide variety of products and services that make up our economy. These companies can be large and have thousands of employees, or they can be small, having only a few employees. Companies can have hundreds of shareholders or can be family owned and run. Any product that can be sold at a higher price makes the company more willing to produce and supply it. A company's decisions are made purely based on how they can maximize their profits.

Profit = Total Revenue - Total Cost

There could be production costs that require capital, on the other hand, there may be no charge of capital required to produce a good. There are instances when a company may choose to capitalize on an opportunity cost, which is when you lose something of value by choosing an alternative. For example, if you choose to splurge on a new car, you will have to give up a vacation to the Bahamas. In layman's terms, this means a trade-off. Most often, companies have to forego some outside opportunities when they redirect their funds to internal projects. They can lose out on earning interest on their savings, for instance, or lose an opportunity to invest in another company.

In addition, there are costs involved when the company uses funds to produce goods or services. Production costs are merely the costs involved in producing or manufacturing the goods that the company wants to sell. All companies want to maximize their profits and minimize their production costs. The reference to the quantity being produced and the materials used to create them is called the production function. Therefore, the cost to produce something can be measured using the production function method to see if they are being efficient in manufacturing goods or providing services. From the production function, you will be able to determine the profit margin between the cost of producing goods and services and selling them.

Pricing the goods is the next step, and setting the price is used as a marketing strategy. Consumers will generally only buy something if they think that the item is worth the price. If they believe that the item is of value to them, you could have a high-profit margin. However, if they perceive the item isn't worth the price, they simply will not buy it. Your company must be able to sustain itself; therefore, the costs should not exceed your sales so that you will be able to make a profit. You can measure the costs using various methods which differ by industry and business model.

Fixed costs are costs that remain the same no matter the quantity of goods produced, and these may include rent, salaries, insurance, or interest repayments. They remain constant for a long period. Variable costs are costs that continuously change depending on the level of the production volume. These costs increase or decrease and depend on whether you make more or less of a product. The average cost is determined by the cost of producing a single unit. This is relatively easy to work out, as you can simply divide the total cost by the number of units produced to get the average cost. Lastly, you have marginal costs. This is the change in the cost to produce one additional unit of a certain product. This includes all costs that differ from the average cost of production.

Monopolies and Oligopolies

Mono olies

A monopoly is a company that is the only seller of a product and the product is one that can't be substituted. A monopoly creates barriers that do not allow other companies to compete with them. These three sources cause these barriers:

1. Resource monopoly - where a single company owns the resource. This type of monopoly is quite rare.

2. Monopolies created by the government - where the company has been given exclusive rights by the government to produce these goods. This is usually done in the interest of the public. Prominent examples include copyright and patent laws, which allow the government to create a monopoly.

3. Natural monopoly - where the cost to produce the goods by a single firm is far more efficient and can be marketed far cheaper than if many companies produced it.

A monopoly can influence the cost of production and the marketing of the product. Its revenue is maximized because the monopoly decides the quantity it will produce and the price it will charge to receive the highest profit. For the owners of the monopoly, this has a favorable outcome. However, this is detrimental to the consumer. A monopoly will always have a higher profit margin because of its power. When a customer pays the monopoly's price, the company is better off and the consumer is worse off by the same amount. The government can get involved by making these industries competitive, making them into public enterprises, or regulating their behavior. Some experts say that it would be better for the government to leave the monopolies alone. However, there have been cases where a monopoly has sold the same products to different consumers at different prices, and this will not be possible if the market is competitive.

Oligopolies

Oligopolies are two or more companies that dominate the market by producing the same type of goods. Oligopolies are usually supermarket and retail chain stores, internet service providers, etc. Even though there is no limit to the number of companies that can be part of an oligopoly, there should be enough firms that one company's decisions can influence the other companies. Usually, competition should then restrict changes in prices as customers will not purchase goods from companies with increased prices if they have an alternative. In general, groups of companies in an oligopoly are quite stable, and can both compete and collaborate with each other. Thus, the companies within an oligopoly are considered interdependent on each other.

However, since oligopolies can use the price of goods to influence other companies, they are capable of some underhanded behavior. When one firm decides to drop its price, there is a possibility that the rival firms will also drop their prices, which can work against the group as a whole but may benefit an individual company. Thus, oligopolies have to be strategic in their decisions; they have to decide whether to compete with their rivals or work with them to generate a consistent pricing scheme. If they collaborate, they may raise or lower their prices in a concerted manner to generate a higher profit margin. This sets up a barrier that prevents new companies from entering the market, which can slow down progress and innovation and be detrimental to customers. Companies in an oligopoly must also choose whether they will be first to implement a new strategy, or whether they will wait to see their rival's strategy and improve upon it. Sometimes having a head start can be more advantageous if they can generate profits before anyone else; at other times, it pays to wait and then improve on the strategy.

Chapter 2:
Discover the Economic Concepts Everyone Uses, but No One Talks About

Economics, at its most basic level, is the study of human behavior. When people are faced with a lack, or too much, of something, they make decisions. These decisions can be family decisions, personnel decisions, or even business and societal decisions. Scarcity is part of life, all you have to do is look around you, and you can't miss it. Humans are always in need of some type of goods or services. There, unfortunately, is not enough to go around. Resources that are needed to produce goods and services are in short supply. Even time, of which everyone has 24 hours, is scarce.

When resources are limited, the number of goods and services we can produce also becomes limited. Now, if you pair this up with everything that humans want, you will understand why the world limited. Even the most developed countries have people who use a park bench as their beds. Not everyone has a place to live or enough food to eat. Most can't even afford healthcare. The resources required to meet these basic human needs are scarce, which leads us to believe that there is a problem with meeting the needs of others, or perhaps with meeting our own needs. Scarcity is a concept that needs to be understood first before understanding economics. Everything we consume that we don't produce by ourselves, we buy with the money we get from working for pay. Many of us never have enough because of scarcity.

In this chapter, we will take a look at the two main types of economics, microeconomics and macroeconomics. Each one will be discussed in-depth and by the end of this chapter, you will be able to distinguish between them clearly.

Microeconomics focuses on households, businesses, and workers, the individuals in the economy. Macroeconomics focuses on inflation, unemployment, and production, as well as imports and exports. Microeconomics and macroeconomics complement each other in the economy. Both perspectives are valuable and useful because they arise from different points of view. They blend together to help us understand the world of economics. Microeconomics looks at each tree, whilst macroeconomics looks at the entire forest.

Microeconomics

Micro comes from the Greek prefix, 'mikro', which means small, therefore microeconomics means small economics. This is the study of the interaction between individuals and companies and how the choices they make are best suited to the resources they have available. It has an effect on taxation levels as well as how individuals spend their money. People with limited amounts of money simply cannot buy whatever they want, nor can they do everything that they want to do. They make decisions on how to maximize their time and money. Businesses do the same, but they make decisions that will give them the best outcome in terms of profit and success in their industry.

Because these principles affect our daily lives, let's take a look at an example. How do you think this supply and demand will affect rent prices if someone is looking to rent an apartment in New York where there is high demand and a limited supply of apartments? The principles of microeconomics explain that this is the reason housing costs are so high in New York. Let's look at how it works. In order to rent the apartment, a person must settle on a budget for rent. If he/she spends too much on rent, then there won't be enough money for other expenses. Based on this information, he/she will form a budget that determines the maximum willingness to pay for the apartment. However, since apartments are in short supply, there will be others who are interested in the same apartment. They may be willing to pay more, which means he/she will have to increase the budget and cut back in other areas. This excess of demand over supply then drives up the price. This is the essence of the theory of supply and demand, which assumes that the buyers and sellers are equal.

This raises the question, what decides how much people are willing to pay? What are the factors that determine how an individual's budget should be spent? Whether they should work or not and what products and services fit their lifestyle? What determines if they will save for retirement or borrow for a current need? This depends on the theory of consumer behavior. We touched on this earlier, as this theory describes how individuals optimize the use of their limited time and money to get the maximum benefits. A similar theory applies to businesses and states that they will use their limited resources to maximize profits. In this way, microeconomics predicts how the public behaves regarding financial and economic transactions.

Yet many questions remain. How are the prices of items decided? Why are some people willing to pay more for them? How do the public's decisions influence pricing? Beyond the fundamental theory of supply and demand, microeconomics can be divided into five main sections.

The first section examines the choices and demands of the consumer. This explains how an everyday consumer, who has limited income, chooses amongst the various goods and services made available to him. Microeconomics believes that people make decisions based on satisfying their own needs and what would bring them the most happiness. This is called rational decision making, and this theory is prominent throughout the field of microeconomics.

Utility, which is also known as individual benefit, is the reason the consumer makes a decision. The consumer will be more inclined to buy a product if they feel that it is beneficial to them. Consumers determine the level of benefit given by different products, and therefore the demand for certain goods is higher than others. However, the utility of something depends on the individual's experience and current needs. Let's look at this example: We all really enjoy pizza, so eating a slice will be satisfying. However, eating the 5th slice of pizza will give you a stomach ache. With each additional slice you consume after the first one, your desire for pizza decreases. Any slice after the 5th will decrease your satisfaction and so you will choose to buy something other than pizza.

The second section of microeconomics focusses on the choices businesses make. What they should produce, in what quantity, and finally, at what price. Given that businesses want to maximize profits, they will make decisions based on market demand and their competitors. If the businesses have lots of competitors in the same market, they don't have much leeway with their pricing. Government regulations may also restrict them.

The third section combines both the consumer's choices and the company's choices. That is to say, this section looks at the decisions and interactions between consumers and companies. A customer decides when to buy a product and at what price, a business decides what it will charge for the product. Both of them make their choices based on the market price and both decide how much will be consumed and how much must be produced.

It is important to note here that the distribution of information between individuals and companies is not always symmetrical. This asymmetrical information distribution means that whoever has better information has an advantage during the transaction. For example, a used car salesman may not reveal everything there is to know about a customer's potential car purchase. On the other hand, a customer may not admit to risky behaviors when buying life insurance. This imbalance of power means the one with more information benefits, such as selling a car at a higher than reasonable price or getting insurance at a lower than appropriate price.

The fourth section of microeconomics explains the supply and demand input theory. This focuses on how companies get the resources they need to produce what customers want.

The fifth section explains welfare economics. This examines the social side of economics, such as how income and money are distributed and how this impacts the well-being of the people. It also looks at how the government may act to influence the economy and thus improve people's quality of life.

Behavioral Economics

People want different things, some want wealth and power, others want happiness and love. Each person makes economic decisions based on what they want. Consumers find themselves in situations where they do not have the option to choose a close alternative to achieve the same end. Thus, people's behavior drives the economy at a fundamental level.

Behavioral economics is the study of the effect of emotional, social, and psychological factors on individuals' economic decisions when they are uncertain. In an ideal world, we would make the best decision that would give us the most satisfaction and greatest benefit. People, when given an option, will always choose the one that they believe will maximize their satisfaction and be the best option for them. This is the rational behavior theory we mentioned earlier. However, behavioral economics says that humans are irrational and are unlikely to make clear decisions. They are easily distracted, emotional, and make decisions that are not in their best interest. Why do people choose A instead of B? Consumers would believe that they were getting a great deal if a product was introduced into the market for $800 and then reduced to $600. But what if the value of the product was $600 in the first place?

We encounter behavioral economics in nearly all aspects of our daily lives. It explains and impacts our behavior so much that we aren't even aware of it. Here are some examples:

1. Hot-Hand Fallacy - this is the belief that someone that succeeds at a random event

will have great success in future attempts at that event. There is no such thing as a "hot-hand."

2. Self-handicapping - a strategy put in place where people avoid putting in effort or won't admit that they worked hard for something to protect their self-esteem. Even though the student studied hard for a test, she tells everyone that she hardly studied for it. She has put an obstacle in her way to preemptively explain why she succeeded or failed.

3. Anchoring - influencing a person's actions by planting a thought in their minds. This is fundamental to the advertising industry.

4. Gambler's Conceit - a belief that a person can stop a dangerous course of action while they are still doing it. For example, a gambler saying that he can stop or that he'll stop when he wins.

5. Rationalized Cheating - this is when people do not think of themselves as bad people. We will more likely take a pen home than the cash equivalent. Rationalizing our actions as opposed to admitting we are stealing.

We think that we have control over our lives and the decisions we make, unfortunately, this is not always the reality. We all make use of both rational and irrational thinking. These concepts are fundamental to microeconomics, and in many ways, can be applied to macroeconomics as well, since macroeconomics as a field arises from everyone's microeconomic decisions.

Macroeconomics

Macroeconomics focuses on the entire economic process, from inflation to unemployment. What are the factors that determine how many goods and services a country needs? What determines how many jobs are available and what the standard of living should be? Why do companies expand and employ more workers and how does the economy grow? Why is macroeconomics so important?

1. Our economic system is quite complicated. Macroeconomics helps us understand how it functions.

2. It analyses and explains economic growth and how we can sustain it. It can also help to achieve a higher employment level and high economic growth.

3. It assists in stabilizing prices in businesses and advises what policies must be put in place to control inflation and deflation.

4. It finds solutions to end poverty, inflation, and unemployment.

5. It has given us a holistic view of economics and has helped us overcome the challenges of microeconomics.

Given that macroeconomics looks at the economy on a much broader scale, that of regions and nations. It looks at things like the standard of living, wealth distribution, or the purchasing power a given country or region has. One of the key measurements within macroeconomics is the output of a country, or how many goods and services are produced. This is quantified based on how much they cost and is called the gross domestic product. In general, countries want to have a high level of output per person as this means the country is prosperous and can maintain a higher standard of living.

The standard of living is measured based on the number of material goods that are available for a person, family, nation, or group. The quality of life is measured by satisfaction, relationships, and freedom. You can also relate the quality of life to the material standards. The standard of living is measured by the value of goods and services produced by everyone in the country in a year. If a country produces a lot of goods, they will be able to pay higher wages, enabling the residents to spend more. Consumer spending makes up to 68% of the US economy. When people spend money on clothing and groceries, it not only improves their lives but it also helps businesses, who in turn hire more workers. A country's residents can also benefit from a higher standard of living when the government spends money on building roads and public transport systems.

The distribution of wealth and income is the way a nation divides its wealth and income amongst the population. Wealth is the monetary value of all accumulated possessions and financial claims. Income is the net total of payments that have been received in a certain period. Income is what someone gets paid, while wealth is everything of value they've collected. Why are some countries richer than others? What can be done to address this inequality? In common terms, being rich means having more wealth and possessions than average. A country that has a higher rate of economic growth enables people to move out of poverty more quickly. People who earn a higher profit are motivated to improve production. On the other hand, people who are not rewarded are least likely to have the incentive to produce. Similarly, high productivity in a country enables quicker economic growth. This allows a country to escape poverty. Government support is needed to develop a country's economy. Nations trade with each other because they have the opportunity to benefit from each other. Thus, governments can foster trade as a way to improve their country's economy.

Purchasing power parity (PPP) is a theory used in economics that compares the living standards between countries. In order to make a comparison across nations, the production of goods and services of different categories must be included. Imported goods will sell at a higher cost than locally produced goods because of transportation costs and import duties. VAT or value-added tax can also increase prices from one country to the next. Higher prices could also be caused by deliberate action from the company to be competitive in their pricing.

Purchase power parity allows for a price comparison between countries and their different currencies. This economic term says that if there are no barriers in the trade market or no transaction costs, then the item should cost the same no matter where you are. Ideally, the shirt you buy in South Africa should cost you the same in England. Purchasing Power Parity can compare the prices of one basket of goods to another basket in a different location my measuring how to what extent factors such as taxes and poverty prevent the purchase of various goods. One mobile, one shirt, and one motorbike should cost the same in the US and in China. Every consumer in every country should have the same power to purchase goods with the right exchange rate. However, even though PPP can compare the cost of goods, it does not include the quality of goods or profits. Organizations use different baskets of goods to compute different results. Thus, price levels and inflation data are measured differently from one country to another.

Chapter 3:
Proven Principles of Economics to Be Successful and Outsmart 99% of the population

Entrepreneurs must have an understanding of economic principles to expand their businesses successfully. Even if their businesses have been successful without the full knowledge of these principles, they will find that as the business grows, problems will arise due to flaws in their processes. If unaddressed, these will grow to a point where it can seem overwhelming to the owner. Long-term business success depends on not only understanding these basic principles but also applying them to their business and marketing strategy. Understanding these principles will answer any questions you may have about your business prospects. Everything from marketing and setting prices to planning your business strategy will be covered.

First, there are five important principles that must be understood in order to analyze business decisions from an economic standpoint. Understanding these principles will allow you to determine which decisions will lead to profit and which will lead to losses for your company.

1. **Risk and return** - Small businesses are risky enterprises. Small businesses have the highest number of shutdowns and bankruptcies. On the flip side, small businesses also have the highest returns for their investors. In the past 70 years, small business stock averaged a 17.7% increase, while the large companies averaged 12.5%. Business owners must acknowledge that their business might fail and include this in their business strategy. The higher the risk that the financial asset has, the higher the return must be in order to attract investors.

2. **Marginal benefits and marginal costs** - The gains from producing an additional product are referred to as the marginal benefits, while the expenses for that extra product are the marginal costs. There is a profit when the marginal benefits are equal to or larger than the marginal cost. However, a loss will be incurred when the marginal cost surpasses the benefits. When they are equal, then the benefit has been maximized and increasing production will only increase costs. When producing a new product, the

marginal cost is always higher than the benefit until enough units can be sold to recoup the production costs, leading to profit. Companies should analyze the relationship between the marginal cost and the marginal benefit for each of the company's activities. If you consider increasing wages, you will have long-term employees, therefore minimizing the training of new employees. Employees that are happy give great customer service. Both of these can increase profit, but if wages are increased further, the benefits may no longer outweigh the costs.

3. **Opportunity costs** - The opportunity cost refers to the comparison between the cost and benefit of the chosen activity compared to the next best option. Small business owners must always consider the opportunity cost when they're growing their business. You have to take into account whether what you're investing in is cost-effective, without jeopardizing another aspect of the business.

4. **Sunk Costs** - These are unrecoverable expenses and should have no bearing on any future decisions once a decision has been made. These include costs such as salaries, rent, or any other expense that

must be paid whether your company has sold lots or little for the month. Fixed costs should be removed when making decisions because you will not be able to get the money for these back.

5. **Supply and demand** - Demand for goods depends on the consumers' preferences and the quantity demanded is based on the price. The quantity of the goods that are needed and their price is called demand. Supply shows how much of the goods are available in the market.

In addition to these principles, 6 essential behavioral economics principles influence the decisions made by business owners as well as customers. Economics is defined as "a social science concerned chiefly with description and analysis or the production, distribution, and consumption of goods and services" (Merriam-Webster, n.d.). Behavioral economics is founded on the observation that economists don't study humans, they study behavior. For decades, the dogma in economics has been that people are rational beings that are consistently calculating what is in their best interest, and they behave accordingly.

Now, with insights from other social sciences, behavioral economists are reshaping the subject of economics. The founder of behavioral economics, Daniel Kahneman, noted, "It seems that traditional economics and behavioral economics are describing two different species" (Kahneman, 2011). The key difference is that human beings in traditional economics are calculating, rational, and objective, but human beings in behavioral economics are emotional, biased, and unpredictable. Behavioral economics impacts all businesses, because challenges in business are challenges that humans face. Businesses must learn to understand consumers and then inspire them. The six fundamental behavioral economics principles for any business are listed below:

The Overconfidence Effect - Humans tend to overrate their performance, and they are very biased when assessing themselves. Humans cannot be objective on lots of matters. People don't exaggerate their abilities because they want to impress, they rather err on the side of self-regard. We all have something called an ego-protective cognitive mechanism. When employees were asked to rate themselves, they generally rated themselves in the top 5% of the company's employees. Over 80% of businesses believe that their customer service is excellent. However, only 8% of their customers agreed. The overconfidence effect implies that a company's brand is not aware of its shortcomings.

Temporal Discounting - Consumers make decisions based on a cost-benefit calculation, according to traditional economics. Temporal discounting is based on the fact that humans prefer to be rewarded immediately rather than wait. If we were offered $5 this month or $10 next month, we would prefer to take the first option. Rewarding customers is an attempt by companies to keep them happy. Customers are prepared to pay double for instant gratification.

Loss Aversion - Most people hate losing more than they love winning, and this describes just how the mind measures the pain of losing against the pleasure of winning. Losing a privilege is far more important than gaining it.

Anchoring and Framing - These are two powerful deviations in our minds. Anchoring is our ability to rely on the first piece of information we have. The first impression we receive determines how we interpret the information we receive after this. Salespeople use this all the time. They suggest an incredibly high price, then allow the customer to negotiate, bringing the cost down considerably. The customer will probably pay what the car is actually worth, but they feel like they got the car at a bargain price. Framing is how choice can influence the outcome. We will eat more when served on a larger dish than a smaller one. Rationally, we should only eat until we're full, it shouldn't matter how big or small our plate is. The framing and anchoring principle are used to manipulate rather than inform the consumer, and this gives the company lots of power and responsibility.

Social Norms - We're all aware of the influences that society has on us; we are not immune to social and peer pressures. We all instinctively conform, and this can be used to promote positive social behavior. The need to fit in is more powerful than we think it is. Build your business on the promise of shared values and align your brand to the social norms that apply to your customers. You'll be more likely to persuade them to use your brand than another brand that fails to connect with their beliefs.

The Peak-End Rule - Humans, without even knowing it, form impressions by relying on the most intense emotional moments they experience. The peak-end rule is used as a guide by companies hoping to give customers a great experience. The customer's journey should have instances of joy throughout the process.

These insights can transform your business by changing the way you approach challenges.

Behavioral economics is rooted in psychological reality. With proper research and guidance, businesses can find strategies that provide solutions to complicated problems as well as strategies that customers can relate to. In this way, they can capitalize on the power of behavioral economics.

Entrepreneurs are all about getting things done and many believe that real-life experience trumps having a degree. Even though experience doesn't always beat knowledge, some business owners have been known to pay young innovators not to get a degree. Theoretical sciences, like economics, can help people prevent many common start-up mistakes. Take a look at these five economic truths:

1. **Value is Subjective** - Entrepreneurs believe that your customers define the value of your product, not you. The value of a good or service is based on how the consumer sees it. To sell your product, you have to give the customers what they want. The cost of the product is not the main determinant of sales.

2. **Demand Curves Slope Downward** - This is also known as the "law of demand" and actually means that the higher the product's price, the fewer products are

sold and vice versa. This is why price skimming works, you can target different customers, at different times, using different pricing.

3. **Price Elasticity is Relative to Demand** - Find your pricing sweet spot. This means that you need to find the ideal point between elasticity and inelasticity. Entrepreneurs know that if your price is high, you will sell fewer products. If you lower the price, you will make more money up to a point. However, if your price is very low, you will no longer be able to recover your production costs and thus lose money.

4. **One Must Consider Opportunity Costs in Terms of Both Competitors and Customers** - Customer satisfaction defines the value of your product. Opportunity cost must be considered rationally. Businesses are not only competing with each other, they're competing with the customers as well. Your product won't be sold if there are better options out there. You need to make sure that your brand stands out from the others.

5. **One Must Maximize Comparative Advantages to Create an Overall Advantage** - Do what you're good at. Comparative advantage literally means that you should do the one thing you're better at even if you're just a little better at it than something else. In any entrepreneurial start-up, talk is cheap, you should be doing something to make ends meet. Economic truths that were relevant 250 years ago are still true today.

These insights will help you make informed decisions and have a better plan to avoid costly mistakes. Use these economic principles to guide your decision-making when determining what products or services you will produce, how you will market them, and who you wish to sell them to.

We've all heard the saying, "There's no such thing as a free lunch". In simple terms, this means that in order to get one thing, you have to give up another. Making a decision is a trade-off. Examples of this range from how someone decides how to spend their money to how a student wants to spend their time. Another example is the trade-off between efficiency and equality. The definition of efficiency is when society gets maximum benefits from scarce resources. An example of this is when the rich pay taxes and the money is given to the poor. Even though this improves equality, it also lowers the incentive for hard work. The definition of equality means a fair distribution of economic prosperity among everyone. This means that the increase in equality is at the detriment of our resources. Economics says that there is another way to look at the world and nothing is black or white. An extra $100 will make a big difference if you earn very little, however, if you earn a very high salary, you won't even notice it.

Economists have a great love for theory, sometimes to the point that they forget that theories must eventually be applied. Entrepreneurs are people of action so they can enjoy the practicalities and the fruits of economic theories. Self-interest makes the world go round. Therefore people respond to appropriate incentives as opposed to vague promises. You cannot depend on people without rewarding them. People very rarely help out without expectations of some kind of compensation. Always try and offer something in exchange for mutual gain instead of charity. Also, keep an eye on how price affects sales in your market. In higher-end markets, a lower price can decrease sales. This is called "goods with snob value" because people buying this item buy it for social status. Customers can also become loyal to a particular brand, so try to build this loyalty to secure your customer base.

While building a new business from the ground up, it's easy to forget that time is your most valuable resource. Outsource whatever you can so that you can focus on high-priority tasks. You don't have to do everything as a company or as an individual. In life, you have hundreds of opportunities to win and one chance to lose. Don't allow uncertainty to discourage you, take a risk, it may just be worth it.

Chapter 4:
The Future of
Entrepreneurship

How Can You Use These Principles to Become Successful?

A sustainable business is a firm that ensures that its business participates in eco-friendly or green activities. They make sure that whatever they do has minimal impact on the environment. A business that follows these principles will be considered green: they have committed to maintaining environmental principles in their business. They have incorporated sustainable principles when making decisions for their business, and they provide and or replace non-green products with eco-friendly ones.

Sustainability is described as a three-legged stool, people, product, profit. Sustainable businesses are forward-thinking in their approach to human rights, treating their employees well and sourcing their materials ethically. These businesses aim to meet the needs of the customer as well as the environment. Their products meet stringent green guidelines while still keeping a healthy profit margin. They aim to meet the customer's expectations without harming the earth. They make a significant effort to eliminate the harmful effects that may come from the production of their products. For example, sustainable businesses and jobs often aim to use clean energy, and in this way, contribute to reducing greenhouse gases.

The most common green initiative is going paperless, but there are many other initiatives, such as using non-toxic materials, eliminating waste, and refurbishing old pieces of furniture. The life cycle costs for the products are also taken into account because this impacts the process used to make them. There is a lot of pressure from governments, shareholders, and consumers to adopt green practices. Green investment companies are attracting much interest and can create far more opportunities to promote sustainable practices. These firms can assist small businesses with loans, business education, and networks for green products.

The origins of green businesses can be traced back to pioneering companies before WWI. Even the owner Ford Motor Company, Henry Ford, experimented with plant-based fuels. The FMC also upcycled a crate that was used as floorboards in the factory. Today Ford vehicles are made in such a way that they can run on sensible fuel.

Another company, Subaru in Lafayette, achieved a zero-landfill status and became the first vehicle manufacturer to do so. Another example is a Korean company that uses rice husks to package stereo equipment, and the husks are later recycled to make bricks. Companies are giving back on a social level as well, their employees volunteer either by giving time or through donations.

Green organizations must sustain the community, customers, and employees for them to be truly sustainable. There are numerous revenue opportunities that companies can take advantage of and some of the innovative strategies include:

1. Developing technology that allows companies to change their products and decrease waste.

2. Forming a network of like-minded companies who partner together to share knowledge.

3. Committing to integrating improved processes to reduce waste.

4. Reporting the company's performance on sustainable goals.

5. Sourcing sustainable products and having a sustainable strategy or business model.

Organizations must integrate social and ethical practices into the management system. It is no longer an option, your business must incorporate sustainability. The world is constantly changing, and having eco-friendly values can be critical to your business's long-term success. The changes in our climate and increasing income inequality are just a few of the problems that need to be addressed. Believe it or not, having a sustainable business strategy addresses both. Sustainable production of goods benefits the environment because consumers purchase those instead of goods produced in an unsustainable way. Meanwhile, sustainable and ethical sourcing of resources and pay for employees helps decrease income inequality.

Your business must be profitable so that it can do good for the environment and community. If you establish a profitable business using a sustainable model, you will be able to protect your company's brand from improper practices. Otherwise, funds spent on public relations are funds that could have been spent on the business itself. Above all, you will be protecting the environment and yourself. Sustainability should not detract your business from its goals, it should instead motivate it with a purpose and drive skilled workers and financial success. Your organization should be a place that does good and not just a place that provides a salary.

Almost everyone has become environmentally conscious and this has affected how they shop. More than 50% of US customers have changed their habits to lower their impact on the environment. Millennials are willing to pay extra for goods made from sustainable ingredients or goods that are socially responsible. There is a huge demand for sustainable products and you can get your share of it if your company commits itself to sustainable practices. Individuals that feel overwhelmed and out of their depth can collaborate with successful companies to find a solution to combat some of the world's problems. Companies that work together can solve problems that the government is struggling with. Having a sustainable strategy certainly does not mean that you have to sacrifice your profits. Quite the opposite, it has instead become crucial to the success of many companies. If your company is not sustainable, you risk losing out on profit and growth.

Recently, Samsung suspended its business dealing with a company in China because of child labor allegations. Oil companies were faced with environmental issues in countries where they operate. These are challenges many business leaders have to face in order to bring sustainability to their business. Today's business leaders are very aware that everything they do is under constant scrutiny and everything about the way the company operates is being displayed to the world via social media. They are basically running their business in a fishbowl. So how can you implement sustainability and what does this actually mean? It's about being smart in your business, not just about doing the right thing.

You must develop practical ways to apply these sustainable principles. They will, in turn, maximize your opportunities and minimize negativities. Sustainability encompasses issues such as corruption, human rights, and climate change, to name just a few. To work towards zero emissions, measures are introduced to minimize pollution and also reduce costs. To address the safety of workers, security policies are being introduced to mines and oil fields. The World Economic Forum's white paper has integrated business sustainability suggestions from experts in different areas. Therefore, it can provide a solid foundation for business leaders to incorporate and develop sustainable policies in their businesses. This resource will be invaluable to private companies, civil society groups, as well as government organizations. The white paper provides a concrete starting point and helps to frame sustainable discussions.

Recently, a large number of organizations have implemented sustainable practices voluntarily. The quick rate at which these principles were adopted started a debate about long-term implications. Was this part of a strategic plan to promote high financial gain? Or was it to ensure that these organizations survived in the long-term? As much as it's necessary for survival, can it be enough to build a competitive advantage? Sustainability is becoming common practice and some companies have adopted this practice to improve their profit margins by exploiting cost efficiencies.

Companies can benefit from common practices because they are recognized as legitimate. Some say that sustainability is being used to generate a competitive advantage that could result in an above-average performance, i.e., doing well by doing good. However, there is a distinction between operational effectiveness and strategy. A strategy is being different by having a unique and valuable position that is difficult to match. Does this mean that sustainability can be spread through imitation, and if so, does it have a low potential for being competitive? As an increasing proportion of companies adopt sustainable practices, these practices are becoming more of a strategic necessity than a strategic differentiator. Adoption must be done earlier rather than later to make them a market leader in the industry. That said, early and effective implementation of sustainable practices has put some companies miles ahead of their competitors.

One way to help make your business sustainable is to start a home-based business. Covered below are some of the benefits of starting a home-based business that contributes to sustainability and increases your probability of success. Starting a business from home gives you a level of flexibility that you won't find if you were to rent or buy office space. Even though it requires much discipline, there can be substantial benefits. Here are a few tips for starting a winning home-based business in a weak economy.

1. The number one benefit is that you won't have to commute to the office and then back home. Your commute will be just a few steps to your home office, leaving you with more time to work on your business and decrease your carbon footprint.

2. You will have the ability to tailor your work hours and office space according to your immediate requirements. You won't have the luxury of this if you sign yourself into a lease. You can hire workers as you need them.

3. You will be able to make a tax deduction on your business income. If your business qualifies, running it from home could be quite lucrative.

4. Having flexible work hours will allow you to work late into the night if need be. You can schedule your business hours around other obligations you have at home. With modern technology, you can communicate with customers at any time.

5. Your overheads will be relatively low as you won't have gas and phone bills, rent, or utilities to budget for. You can afford to be more generous in your pricing or if you choose to, or you can keep your prices and increase your profits.

6. You have room to test out your business to determine whether it's viable before creating overheads you may not be able to afford. Over 50% of start-up businesses fail within the first year, and if you have fixed costs, this can be a costly failure.

Any individual who creates a start-up or new business is considered an entrepreneur. He or she takes all the risks and benefits from almost all the rewards. Entrepreneurs are innovators with new ideas, products, and business procedures. They play a valuable role in the economy by using their initiative and skills. Entrepreneurs who are successful in risk-taking are rewarded with growth opportunities, high profits, and sometimes even fame. They are integral participants in the economy and offer goods and or services for profit. They face three common and challenging obstacles: overcoming bureaucracy, hiring talent, and obtaining financing. Many use their own money as funding, while others partner with someone who has access to capital. The meaning of the word "entrepreneur" comes from the French verb, *entreprendre*, which means to undertake. They are responsible for creating new things in the pursuit of profit while revealing knowledge. They break tradition and create social change. Successful entrepreneurs have all followed these five general steps:

1. Ensure Financial Stability - This is highly recommended but not an absolute requirement. Having an adequate amount of cash will ease the pressure of making quick money, giving you more time to build a business.

2. Build a Diverse Skill Set - Keep learning and trying new things. If you're building a financial company, learn the sales part of the business as well. This will be handy in tough situations.

3. Consume Content Across Multiple Channels - Read, listen to podcasts, attend lectures, or take short courses. Familiarize yourself with what is going on in the world around you, allowing you to look at your business with new eyes.

4. Identify a Problem to Solve - Identify problems, then find a solution for them. Look at businesses as an outsider. Sometimes we're too close to see the problems.

5. Solve that Problem - Successful businesses add value to a specific problem by solving the problem.

You might have heard this being said before, "Find a way to get paid for the job you'd do for free." This is one of the most important keys to being your own boss. Interact personally with customers, you get honest feedback this way. 80% of business consists of repeated customers, so appreciate existing ones. Answer the phones personally instead of having a generic automated system. Finding the perfect fit takes time as well as trial and error so don't be afraid to tweak if needed. This is an exciting career path and the draw is being your own boss. Do enough research and make sure to include yourself in this. Have an exit strategy in the event your venture does not pan out.

Entrepreneurial economics studies the entrepreneur in the economy. It combines the human creative mind with productivity to provide profitable outcomes. Therefore, entrepreneurship should be encouraged to ensure steady growth in the economy and to develop the long-term economy. Entrepreneurs are the ones creating new industries with their innovative ventures. Economists are theory-driven and aim to model the current state of affairs, but entrepreneurs are now challenging these principles with their achievements, attitudes, and personalities. An entrepreneur is a super manager because of all the functions he performs within the firm, and he reaps the reward for his keen insight and judgment. The entrepreneur is regarded as the missing link as they invest their knowledge into production and they add value to the economy.

Bricolage is another principle that is beneficial in the entrepreneurial world. The word "bricolage" is a French word and means do it yourself. It is essential to address all new tasks immediately. Bricolage is used to explain the process of using all the tools and processes that are available at any given moment to solve the problem. It produces effective results in a world that is constantly changing. To keep a business lean is to work with what you have. Bricolage helps in bringing the focus back to the problem. Many entrepreneurs are distracted by what they would like to achieve in an ideal world. Bricolage is the idea of learning to fix problems themselves, and this idea has been around even before it had its own name. Have you ever heard someone say, "I'll do it myself"? Use bricolage to guide a conversation back to what is available and this will produce cost-effective solutions almost immediately. It is used to maintain the product and keep it constant. Bricolage has reached solutions in ways that businesses have never done before. This is because bricolage can only work with what is available within the business.

The upside of using this principle is that it brings cost-effectiveness and problem-solving to the fore as well as maximizing resources that already exist without duplicating work. There are potential downsides to this as well, bricolage focuses largely on discovery and not on creation. While focusing on only one solution, a business may miss another more lucrative opportunity. This type of thinking will probably face some kind of resistance from leadership if they feel that this is too restrictive. However, this works well with new businesses and entrepreneurs who are able to sustain the business personally. To some, preserving the business mission is key and they will not accept anything that turns their focus away from that just for the sake of practicality. Bricolage may not be the best solution in every situation, but it certainly does offer a different perspective. Keep this in your business toolbox, you never know when this will come in handy.

Chapter 5:
Applying Economic Principles to Today's World

The presence of the internet has certainly changed the way we approach the business world. Industries across the various platforms have merged technology with the traditional ways of doing business. Consumers are exposed to all kinds of virtual goods through the internet. It is estimated that 65% of young school children will have careers that don't exist today. Perhaps even in industries that don't exist yet. Entrepreneurs are also adapting to the new digital age. Digital networking has increased customer potential and has exposed businesses to new ideas through the internet. This may be the best new avenue to choose for entrepreneurs going forward.

There are multiple reasons for the growth of online entrepreneurship, and key among them is that more people can be reached, especially within millennial start-up cultures. With a constantly changing economy, many people have found that traditional jobs are less stable. With the high cost of living and more people going online, there is an abundance of opportunities and inspiration for budding entrepreneurs. It's easier than ever to know what the consumers want as you have direct contact with them. There has been a steady rise in individuals starting up their own business, and with the availability of networking websites and internet-based business models, entrepreneurs have the data they need to inspire innovation.

Entrepreneurs come from all sectors and extremely diverse backgrounds. They are starting at a younger age and are having a radical effect on the digital business world. A recent study showed that even though 95% of entrepreneurs have a Bachelor's degree, only a fraction of them have attended either business school or have any kind of formal business qualification. Entrepreneurship has never been this easy. The abundance of available online resources means that anyone can learn the skills they need to manage a business and build a network.

Not only are start-up businesses accessible, but in today's economy, the start-up business culture is far less volatile and is isolated from the downturns that affect traditional businesses. Millennials are creating jobs for themselves in a new economy instead of looking for jobs in a struggling one. With each new start-up, there are many different opportunities to succeed. As the convenience of online businesses increases, innovation within the digital world will accelerate. Advances in online platforms allow businesses and their employees to streamline their workflows. This makes more room for modern approaches and new methods for entrepreneurs.

Entrepreneurs are not only striving forward through online exposure to potential customers. They are using the cost affecting model of working remotely. The proportion of people working remotely is growing at an exponential rate. The future of new businesses and new business leaders is the digital revolution. Future entrepreneurs will be focused on operating on a global scale and engaging with online perspectives from around the world. As technological advancements spread throughout the globe, they will draw the younger, digitally-inclined generations toward digital entrepreneurship. So, what is digital entrepreneurship, and how can you get started? As digital entrepreneurship grows and as the internet becomes more accessible, this chapter will cover what you will need to embark on this new and exciting platform.

Digital Entrepreneurship

Did you know that 47% of the global population is connected to the internet and 40% of them are active on social media? What about how e-commerce has grown by 49% within the last year? Venturing online is extremely worth it! Some of the most frequently asked questions include: Is it safe? Will I be able to stand out? How do I enter this market? Let's address this common misconception first; there is no such thing as a "making money on the internet while you sleep" magic formula. You have to be willing to work hard and study the markets to ensure that you offer quality products and services to your potential clients. Here are a few tips that can help you. Starting out as a digital entrepreneur is fairly easy; all you'll need is a computer and access to the internet.

Getting Started

To set yourself apart from your competitors, you will need:

Curiosity - Show interest by asking questions. Learn as much as you can about a certain subject. Children are always asking questions. They are curious about the world around them. We need to be like them and try to get an understanding of the way something works. As adults, we simply forget to ask because we're always performing. Cultivate a curiosity about the internet. After all, you will need to understand it to found a business within it. Research is the only way you will be able to know consumer behaviors; it will show you what consumers are struggling with and thus help you find a solution that will add value to their lives.

Become Specialized - Knowledge is constantly changing, ignoring it could adversely affect what you're trying to achieve. People who study for a while and then think that they know everything miss out on valuable information. In simple terms, if you are curious but you're not too keen on studying, then digital entrepreneurship is probably not for you. That being said, you shouldn't spend hours scouring the internet for any and all information. You need to find a balance between learning and implementing this knowledge. After gaining a general foundation of knowledge, choose which niche you will specialize in. Read about your market of choice for about an hour a day and familiarize yourself with how this market operates. This will have a great positive impact on your business.

Help People - Entrepreneurship is mostly associated with identifying problems and finding solutions that have a positive impact. implementing new ideas that are innovative in ways that have never been done before. Let's take a look at Uber. What is so innovative about a taxi service? Nothing. The service they offer is not about getting people from A to B. Instead, they are innovative because their service is practical and easily accessible. Your focus should be on simple solutions with a massive positive impact, that is where your focus needs to be from now on.

h Become a igital Entrepreneur

So it seems like running an online business is something you could do, but what exactly do you gain by choosing this over other start-up options? The answer is simple: freedom, cost savings, and ease of doing business. If you have access to the internet, you will be able to manage your business anywhere. You will make your schedule, meaning you can make time for what you value in life. Finally, since the internet is worldwide, scaling your business and reaching your customers becomes trivial. Let's look at each of these in a bit more detail:

Flexible Hours - When you start your business, you will be working hard and long hours to get the business off the ground. No one can be productive all the time, so working hard does not mean that you have to be working all day long. By defining your schedule, you will become more efficient. You can be flexible in your work hours to spend time with family or allow for unforeseen circumstances.

Cost Savings - Your start-up costs will be at a minimum. By working from home, you save on rent, utilities, and even taxes. The space you occupy will vary according to your business needs but is typically significantly less expensive for digital businesses than traditional brick-and-mortar stores.

Easy Access to Your Target Market - More than 50% of the world's population uses the internet. Starting an online business is the way to go to reach more people. A physical store has mobility and geographical limitations, while digital businesses can reach the world. By targeting your advertisements, you can make sure that you reach your customers, no matter where they live.

Easily Scalable - You can scale your business by increasing production and sales without increasing your marginal costs. This does depend on your personalized business model, but ultimately it will be easier to scale a digital business than a physical one. For example, if you choose to design online courses, you will never run out of stock, and anyone who pays for it will be able to access it immediately. With a physical classroom, you have to pay to rent space, to furnish a classroom, to print materials, and you must go where the students are.

hat Can ou o as a igital Entrepreneur

The next step will be to decide exactly what you'd like to do as an entrepreneur. Your creativity really only limits potential answers, but here are some of the most common options:

Producer - These are individuals who develop content that can be used online. The content can come in various formats, like podcasts, online courses, e-books, etc. All you would need to become a producer is useful knowledge that you would like to share with others.

Affiliate - These are professionals who promote 3rd party goods for commission. This is a great business option for those who don't want to create their own content but who already have online influence.

E-commerce - This type of commerce is where products are sold online and delivered to the customer's home. This business model has changed the way people buy goods and has been steadily increasing in popularity.

Technological Solutions - Start-ups are businesses that are birthed online but can migrate to the physical world if needed. Once again, you must identify a problem that the consumers are faced with and find a simple, easy to understand solution for this.

Digital Influencer - There is no limit to digital influencers, and they often don't have a niche. It is commonly known as the profession of the moment. An example of this is a blog or YouTube channel about make-up. Brands that want to reach your audience will want to create a partnership, often through sponsorships. Influencers can also run ads or use affiliate links to make money, essentially more views and clicks make you more money.

How to Build Your Business

You've now decided what you want to do, but what are the concrete steps you should follow to get started? Some of the best and worst lessons are learned through experience, and although no amount of preparation can prepare you for everything, there are steps that you can take to make sure your business does not end before it gets off the ground.

Identify Your Strengths - What are your strengths? If you're not too sure, try the SWOT method: Strengths, Weaknesses, Opportunities, Threats. This is very easy and simple for you to use as a guide. Use this like you would a pros and cons list. Divide a page into four columns, and then each column into two, essentially having two columns for each heading. Under each heading, write down the positive impact and the negative impacts for your business. This may seem like a tiresome exercise, but by the end, you will have a much better idea of where in the market you are most likely to succeed.

Choose What Type of Product You Would Like to Offer - Now that you know what you are good at, you can find the perfect niche. A niche is a specific market segment, such as the birthday cake segment of the baking industry. Choose something you have a bit of knowledge in and something that you enjoy doing. This way, you can capitalize on the strengths you identified earlier to become an expert. For example, you may have a hobby that you are skilled at and enjoy teaching to your friends. If you base your business around this, then you will likely find the process quite intuitive and enjoyable. The most important question of all is, if you had a choice, what would you like to do for the rest of your life?

Next, find out if there is a demand for what you are offering. Would you be able to make a comfortable living from this? Do a bit of research to see what the demand is for what you're offering. Be aware of what is trending. Just like how we change the way we dress depending on the season, many trends are transient and will fade with time. So you will need to keep a keen eye on market shifts and be prepared to adapt if you choose to pursue something just because it is a current trend. Otherwise, focusing on something with a constant level of demand can give your business more stability and may be preferable as you're just starting out.

Analyze the Market as Well as Your Competitors - Get to know your competition and know them well. This helps you gain some insight as to how they operate and how you can find a competitive edge. Visit your competitors' sites or other similar sites, and focus on what's relevant to your target market. Take note of how they interact with their customers and what they communicate to them. Remember, you are gathering information only. You don't want your business to be a carbon copy of another. Ideally, you would like to improve upon the template they provide so that your business stands out.

Create a Financial Plan - An online business is cheaper than a physical one, but you will need to save up or otherwise acquire some capital before starting up. Get a handle on your personal finances, such as how much you spend in a month, and build up savings in case your business is not profitable right away. Have a detailed plan for what costs will be associated with the materials or equipment you will need, with designing your online platform, with advertising your goods, and with the day to day running of your business such as paying employees or utility costs. Determine what financial targets you will need to hit in order to break even, and anything you make beyond that will be your profits. This information will then be used to determine your sales targets based on the price of your goods.

Get a Domain - If you are creating content or a virtual store, this should be the first step. Choose a domain name that will accurately represent your business. Keep it short and easy to remember so that potential customers can find your page. Visit register.com or godaddy.com to see if your business name has already been chosen. If your product is digital, you don't necessarily need to buy a domain as there are online platforms that you can use to advertise your product.

Make a Prototype of Your Idea - To know whether your idea is feasible, ask yourself these questions: What problem does your product solve? Is it easy to understand? Will it be better than your competitors' products? Would you be willing to buy your product?

Review your plan if you answered "no" to any of these questions and find ways to improve your plans. You should be able to make the necessary improvements to give you a higher chance of success when your product is ready to be launched.

Promote Your Business - It is time to promote your product. Have a good strategy to start advertising your product and to deliver it to your customers. Show them the value of what you are offering. The right audience will pay for it. Soon there will be more than 2.7 billion people using social media. However, not all of them will be part of your target audience. Your communication should be directed towards those who are likely to be interested in your products, and even though you can reach more people, try not to. No matter which platform you choose to use, make your content specifically for that platform.

There are many ways you can reach potential customers. Having an email list is an invaluable asset to any business owner. Make sure you create one of your own instead of purchasing one. Advertising is another great way to impact potential customers; just ensure you have good quality images and great content. Advertise on multiple networks to increase your product visibility. You may also benefit from having your own social media pages, where you create quality content and answer questions honestly. This will help potential customers become comfortable enough to start buying your product. Great content quality will bring lasting results as this builds relationships between you and the customer. Not all marketing types are optimal for every niche, so experiment a bit and find out what works for you.

A Short message from the Author:

Hey, are you enjoying the book? I'd love to hear your thoughts!

Many readers do not know how hard reviews are to come by, and how much they help an author.

I would be incedibly thankful if you could take just 60 seconds to write a brief review on Amazon, even if it's just a few sentences!

Thank you for taking the time to share your thoughts!

Chapter 6:
The Secret to Earning Income with Recycled and Upcycled Materials

Businesses of any size can make a difference for the environment, and there's nothing wrong with making a little money on the side while doing this. This chapter will give you practical advice to realize your dream of starting an ethical business. There are many ethical businesses you could start, and we will talk about a few more in later chapters, but for now, we will look at how you can base a business around recycled and upcycled materials.

Did you know that you can make ends meet by repurposing used clothes, newspapers, plastic, etc.? Many people have learned how to turn recycled trash into a thriving sustainable business. This has become a global mega-trend as over 90% of the world's customers want eco-friendly or environmentally friendly products. Eco-friendly items have seen an increase in sales each year, and sustainable fashion has increased by 75%. This not only helps save the planet, but it is also extremely profitable. Consumers are willing to pay more for repurposed, eco-friendly items. You can turn your concern for the environment into ideas that will fill your wallet. Learn about the thousands of craft ideas that use recycled materials, how to stand out on social media, and how to promote your business on all social media platforms and craft markets.

Curbside collection has supplied a tremendous amount of recycled materials, from paper to glass, and recycling has become an economic system all of its own. The collection of these recyclables outweighs their market value. As the demand for recycled materials grows, it has turned into a competitive advantage for farsighted businesses. With the regulations governing environmental issues becoming tighter, companies have strategically formed alliances with community groups and public organizations. Managers of some of the world's high profile companies such as Coca-Cola and American Airlines have invested in repurposed products and have found that it's in their best interest to do so. They have increased their profits and cut down on waste products. The value of recycling is long-term and makes perfect economic sense.

With everyone jumping onto the green bandwagon, certain misconceptions must be dispelled, such as recycled products being of poor quality and costing more. Businesses that are becoming sustainable by adapting to the new eco-friendly market are providing solutions to their customers. A report by the Retail Industry Leaders Association (RILA) estimated that 68 million Americans would spend at least 20% more on eco-friendly products, and base this on their personal values regarding the environment. Another survey concluded that 87% of US millennial social media users would pay more for sustainable products. Technology has also played its part in providing forward-thinking green initiatives by cloud-based storage and barcode scanners.

The newest trend in sustainability is upcycling, the reusing of materials and objects that have been discarded. Products of a higher quality and value can be created using textile waste. Yarns and materials created by using plastic bottles have become an eco-centric trend. These materials are used to make clothing and accessories. High profile fashion houses are also getting involved. Tommy Hilfiger has launched a line of 100% recycled cotton jeans in 2019, and Adidas has made 6 million pairs of shoes by upcycling plastic collected from the ocean. Sustainability and upcycling in the retail industry are here to stay. Retailers and brand houses need to be innovative to remain relevant to a growing eco-conscious market.

Upcycling, in layman's terms, really means taking something that is slightly dated and making it better by either fixing it or changing it. So, what can you upcycle? Well, anything! Start by painting an old antique replica or even an old chair. A fresh coat of paint can take a tired old piece of furniture and turn it into something new and exciting. Any item that needs a bit of fixing up can be refreshed with your DIY tools. Upcycling is quick and easy, especially with all the products available on the market for these tasks. The transformation of a product from tattered to valuable is more appreciated when it has a rags to riches story behind it. This opens up another avenue for marketing recycled and upcycled goods. Transforming an old airbag into a backpack, or a mosquito net into a sleeve for a laptop, creates what is known as a product biography and gives the product a brand new identity. Recycling is commonly practiced, but now upcycling is becoming more popular and is in such demand that even established companies incorporate it into their business strategy. The psychology behind this is that the customer feels special when a product has a storytelling ability. Value is generated from what would otherwise be considered a waste product, by reshaping and prolonging its life.

As much as there are similarities between recycling and upcycling, there are also differences. Recycling is the breaking down of old materials into raw materials before they can be transformed and repurposed. Upcycling takes an old or outdated item and transforms it by giving it a new identity.

The Skills You'll Need to Sell Products Online.

Now that you've got some ideas of what you can craft out of recycled items or what you might upcycle, you'll need to know how to sell your products. There are plenty of resources available online that you can use to sell your products, and we'll get into the specifics in the next section. First, let's go over the skills and beneficial habits you'll need to develop to become a successful online entrepreneur. It seems obvious, but you must be comfortable online and on the internet, love what you do, and practice to hone your skills. Keep a record or document the steps you've taken so that you can repeat them at a later stage. Know your target market and display your work on as many sites as you can to get more views. Invest in a good camera to ensure that your photos are a good representation of your products. Have excellent customer service and fair pricing. The demand for well made and cleverly designed products has increased dramatically over the last few years, and consumers are looking for one of a kind items as opposed to something mass-produced. To be successful, you need to combine your talent and intuition and then commit yourself to become a professional.

This chapter will be your guide to getting your online business off the ground. You will learn how to promote your craft and sell yourself as a crafter. You will be able to establish your very own website and set up a business system that will propel you into success. Everyone wants to be their own boss and to make millions doing what they love, but before you can embark on the amazing journey, ask yourself if this is right for you. Do you have the right traits to establish and run a successful online store? Entrepreneurs are creative thinkers; they are ready to solve problems, find new opportunities, and take advantage of what's available. Ask yourself the following questions:

1. Can I research my competition and their work and make adjustments to mine to create a better product?

2. Will my creations be popular with the customers, and will I enjoy my hobby as a job?

3. Do I have the time and money to spend to get this business up and running?

4. How much capital do I have to sustain myself in the start-up phase?

5. Will my prices be competitive enough to generate a customer base and income?

Online businesses are generally a one-man show, so you will need to do all the tasks required to run your business and to make it a success. You have to be organized and focused, motivated and productive, market your products and make them better if needed. You need to have a quick response time because customers have no way to interact with you apart from the messages on your site. Respond to questions and queries within 24 hours. Be polite and courteous in your responses and acknowledge messages even when you don't have an immediate answer. Keep the communication going, from the initial query to the order that has been sent out. Your customers will determine the kind of service that is expected of you. Listen to them and take note of everything they say, from thank you to criticism.

The Steps to Start Selling Online

Hobbypreneurs are people who've turned their hobby into a successful business by marketing themselves on a global platform such as Etsy.

This has become a simple and popular way of generating an income from your hobby. Most people want to know which hobby can make you money, and the answer is: your hobby. All you need is some creative thinking and good business sense and you could be on your way. Anything sells, from knitting beanies to woodwork, from jewelry-making to kitchenware, there are endless possibilities. Put a price tag on your hobby. However, if your hobby is skateboarding, it would be difficult to skateboard daily and see your bank balance increase. You need to audit your hobbies to see which one has the greatest potential to make money. Don't count anything out; sometimes the least likely hobbies will have the highest money-making potential. Do some research, and remember that it is very likely that someone else is selling a similar product, so compare pricing and see what the best-sellers are. Most online stores are saturated with similar products, so you need to find a way to set yours apart. Hobbies are supposed to be fun, so if you're no longer having fun, it's no longer a hobby.

Figure out where to source the products you would like to sell. Try contacting those in your community, as using local materials can have a great positive impact on both your surroundings and business. Selling online can seem quite daunting at first. It's fairly easy to set up, so don't worry about it being too costly or taking too long. Have a plan for selling, either through a marketplace, on social media, or your very own store. Once you have the products you will sell, you need to attract the customers. There are many ways to sell to an online market. The four most common ways are listed below, and the great thing is that you don't have to choose one or the other. You can use them all.

1. **E-commerce stores:** This allows you to integrate your online store with social media or marketplace. You can use the apps provided by Facebook, Amazon, etc., to link your store in such a way that you can sync your products, so whoever visits your Facebook page will see the products that you have on your online store. It is very easy to manage, and you can update your business and all social media platforms so they are updated automatically as well. You can manage your business with your smartphone from anywhere at any time. You are always in control of how your online store looks and feels, and you can control your products' presentation. You can make changes that you feel are necessary without waiting for Facebook or Amazon. Your sales can be processed quickly and your products

can be showcased faster than before, leaving you to focus on the more important parts of your business. You are able to literally run a 24-hour store. The top three e-commerce platforms are:

a. Shopify

b. Wix

c. BigCommerce

Your store can be successful no matter which platform you choose to use. They are all designed to promote your product. You first need to create an account before you can start selling. Use the free trial period to test out the platform before committing to it and paying the monthly fee to use it. Building your own online store makes you look like a professional, which makes you a credible seller. You must build trust in the online shopping community for them to buy from you. E-commerce platforms have two excellent reasons for you to use them to sell online: abandoned cart recovery and mobile responsiveness. The abandoned cart recovery allows you to contact customers who have not yet confirmed their order for whatever reason, giving you another chance to close the sale. Over 39% of online shoppers use their mobile phones to place an order in an average month. Your store must work well on a mobile as well as a desktop. E-commerce platforms are automatically designed to work on mobile. So, no matter how big the screen is, buying your products will run smoothly. E-commerce platforms can be compared to a Swiss army knife, where you have lots of tools easily and readily available from one platform.

2. **WordPress:** They started out as a blog publishing system. In the last few years, they've begun to support web content and have become one of the most popular platforms in the content solutions industry. This is a great option for an online store. Here are some easy steps to get started with WordPress: Choose a product that you would like to sell and decide on what the niche will be, digital or physical products. Buy a domain name which, in simple terms, means a URL and add an extension, typically .com or .net. Make sure that it is easy to remember and easy to say. Keep in mind that non-profit organizations use the extension .org. Keep the domain name short. Use acronyms if your name is long because your site will gain popularity more quickly if the domain is easy to remember.

The next step is to obtain a host for your site. Luckily, WordPress offers hosting packages, making it very convenient since everything is available in one place. Note that if you plan to set up your site elsewhere, make sure that you sign up with a reputable host with great customer service. When you are one hundred percent sure of your choice, sign yourself up. Once you've downloaded WordPress onto your site, you will have a walkthrough guide to get you through all the technical stuff. Now that you have your WordPress site set up and your products are all lined up, it's time to start selling. Choose an e-commerce platform. Now it's time to make sure that the site is working the way it should. Go through the processes as a customer to ensure that any problems are ironed out before going live. Check that all the digital files have been uploaded correctly, you may also want to check the download speed. Don't forget about your emails. See if the wording and branding are correct before you start advertising.

3. **Marketplaces:** Selling on marketplaces such as Amazon, Etsy, and eBay is great for people who want to sell their product quickly and don't mind competing with millions of other people. Amazon has over

two million sellers and is extremely popular. For you to sell on these marketplaces, all you need to do is create an account and list the products you wish to sell, along with the price and description. Accept payment and ship the goods. It's that easy. You can enter the marketplace quite easily as there is little to no barrier to entry. Etsy and Amazon have a huge number of customers that will ensure that you can immediately start selling. The trick though, is for you to stand out from the crowd of other sellers. You cannot rely on the marketplace to promote your product. In fact, Amazon searches are constantly changing, so your product will be visible one day but not the next. You must have a unique brand that allows you to stand out so that you're not one of many sellers promoting the same product. There will almost always be someone new on the market with a lower price that will take the customer away from you. A trustworthy brand can be a valuable asset in the long-term. Marketplaces do charge a fee, so read the fine print before you commit.

By selling on Amazon, you are using their reputation to sell your goods. Everything from DVDs to electronics is sold on this platform. Amazon is so popular that you may find yourself in competition with Costco or Walmart. Amazon's fees are based on what you're selling as well as the quantities sold. For a little bit extra, they will provide you with a delivery service.

Etsy is a platform used mainly by artists and crafters and thus can be a great choice for sustainable crafts. The customers are more focused on a specific type of product. Buyers and sellers are like-minded, so they don't mind spending a bit more on an item. Etsy also charges a fee, so remember to check it out before signing up.

You can sell almost anything and everything on eBay, therefore it's almost impossible to build a business here. Because eBay is structured on a bidding model, customers are not obligated to pay you until the time runs out, and until then you will not be sure how much money you will receive. Also, check out their fees, eBay charges 10% of what you've sold.

4. **Social media sites:** With over two billion users, Facebook is currently the biggest social media site in the world, and you can use this platform to match your product to the consumer easily. Before you can get started, you must create a business

page. Facebook is a bustling platform, so don't expect a response by just posting your product. Find a way to hold the customers' attention. Run promotions and give out discounts, ask questions, and use videos and jokes if you have to. Don't undersell your page, post regularly to get enough traffic through your page to make it stand out. Link your Facebook page to an e-commerce platform and you will be able to manage your inventory and products in one place. If you choose to sell exclusively via Facebook, this can be quite time-consuming as all orders will have to be handled manually.

Now that you know which platform you will be using, putting together a business strategy is the next step. Getting an online business off the ground can be a bit tricky and seem daunting. Most of these we touched on before, but make sure you have answers to the following questions:

1. How many products must I sell to make a profit and how will I achieve this?

2. What would it cost to buy or produce an item and have it delivered to the customer?

3. Keep it simple and do some research on your competitors. After all, you're learning as you go. Who are your competitors?

4. What are consumers spending their money on and can I match their needs to my products?

5. Will potential customers be able to find my products online?

Having the right customer for your products is critical to success, so you need to supply products that someone needs. To determine what products are most likely to sell, take a look at what the most successful companies are advertising. Provide products for the market and don't look for a market for a product. It does not matter how good your online store looks, or how professionally you handle business, you are not going to sell if no one's interested in what you are selling. Ensure that there is a demand for your product. Since you will be selling your own creations, much of the draw lies in the personal touch.

So, what will sell online? Wouldn't it be nice to know what products will be trending in the next few months? If there was a way to do this, we'd all be multi-millionaires. One thing that you can do now that you have a product in mind is a google trend search. This is a great tool that will enable you to see what's trending and what's not. Search a few options and take a look at the most popular and trending product results. This will give you a heads up on what to offer your customers. If you take note of the spikes, you will also see when the best time would be to increase your sales.

Online forums are also a great way to find out what customers are thinking about. Reading online forums can be like having a million or so customers telling you what they think and what can be changed in a product. The key though, is to sell what you love and what you are passionate about. It will be easier to sell something you enjoy. However, don't overlook the money-making potential of another product. The next step would be for you to source the raw materials at a reasonable price. Contact wholesalers or retailers and find out if you can put your brand on them, especially if you will be bulk buying and storing. You can also look for individuals in your local community who may be willing to work with you, such as contractors who may have scrap wood or plastic waste you can repurpose.

Chapter 7:
The Complete Guide to Producing Your Own Food for Profit

You've probably heard or read about the bio-integrated system of aquaponics. This chapter will cover the basics of this process. The combination of two different main elements, fish farming and plants growing in a water source, is the basis of aquaponics. The interaction between the two provides benefits for both to thrive. The fish waste in the water provides the plants with the nutrients they need for healthy growth. The plants use the nitrogen from the water and this, in turn, purifies the water for the fish. This creates a self-sustaining system that generates plant and animal produce. Aquaponics reduces problems that aquaculture and hydroponics have when used alone. Growing huge quantities of fish place a strain on the water they're being grown in. The water becomes polluted with chemicals and waste from the fish, necessitating constant maintenance. Plants grown hydroponically need fertilizer to grow because the water does not have enough nutrients to sustain them. This is how aquaponics works to overcome these challenges:

1. The fish enrich the water with their excrement.

2. The bio-filter circulates the water.

3. The plants grow quite quickly as a result of the nitrates in the water.

4. The water that goes back into the fish tank is pure and oxygenated.

This cycle benefits both the fish and the plants. However, we have yet to mention the third and most important part of this system: microorganisms. These microorganisms make the nitrogen cycle possible and more efficient. To have a successful aquaponic system, you need to use nitrifying bacteria because a mechanical filtration system can't filter out all the ammonia from the water. Biofilters get rid of decaying matter that has dissolved in the water through physical filtration. The microorganisms within the filter then convert the excess ammonia and nitrite to nitrate, which the plants use to grow happily.

Can you imagine being able to grow your own food? You can raise your own fish and grow your favorite vegetables, and there's very little work involved. Aquaponics systems are becoming quite popular and almost everyone wants one. Professional and pre-made aquaponics systems can be costly to buy. Therefore many have resorted to building their own. There are loads of really diverse systems from the simple DIY to the more professional hi-tech systems. There are considerable benefits to having a system like this in your home. Here are a few of them:

1. Aquaponics husbandry eliminates weeds and tiny insects from your garden.

2. The nutrients in the water are continually being circulated, so none of the nutrient-rich water is lost.

3. Aquaponics conserves water by using about 1/10th of the water required by other systems. This is a great advantage in areas where there is a shortage of water.

4. The ecosystem is natural, so no harmful chemicals or pesticides will be used.

5. The system is space-efficient so you can place it anywhere and in any room inside or outside your home.

6. This system can be scaled to your requirements.

7. You can get fresh, nutritious food that's free from toxic chemicals.

Even though aquaponics is a very simple system, you do need some know-how if you plan on making one. Here is a list of equipment you will need to make a simple aquaponics system:

Tools:

- A drill
- Drill bits: 3/16", ½" and ⅞."
- A hacksaw
- A pipe cutter
- Razorblade
- Cutters
- Thread seal tape

Materials:

- 15-gallon plastic grow bed
- ½" irrigation tubing
- 2 ½" ball valves
- 3 ½" barb adapter
- ½" flex pipe tee insert
- ½" MNPT X barb 90-degree elbow
- 2 x #14 O-rings
- 2" PVC pipe 8 ¾" long
- 2" PVC cap

- 1 ¼" PVC pipe 6 ⅝" long

- 1 ¼" PVC cap

- ½" PVC pipe 5 ⅝" long

- ½" male adapter

- ½" female adapter

- 2 ½" PVC pipe 3" long

- 2 ½" 90-degree elbows

- Hydroponic rock and pea gravel combination

- 30-gallon plastic fish tank

- Black plastic sheeting

- Plastic storage shelves

- 100 - 130 GPH submersible pump

How to build the automatic siphon:

1. Insert the ½" pipe into the ½" male adapter.

2. Drill a hole at the bottom of the grow bed and pass this through the hole with an O-ring. This will ensure that there are no leaks from the grow bed.

3. Attach the male adapter from the outside to the female adapter.

4. The two 90-degree elbows and the 3" PVC pipe are then inserted into the adapter, making up the drainage assembly.

How to build the water pump system:

1. Secure the pump to a paving stone using a zip tie.

2. Using a barbed tee fitting, run the ½" irrigation tubing from the motor.

3. Attach a piece of irrigation tubing and threaded adapter to this and screw in a ball valve.

4. Attach a longer piece of irrigation tubing to the other barb, then attach a threaded adapter, a ball valve, and another threaded adapter.

5. Add more irrigation tubing and the 90-degree elbow fitting. The ball valve will control the water flow.

How to test the system:

1. Place the system in its designated area and fill your tank with water.

2. Secure the water inlet for the grow bed. Carefully plug in the water pump as per the directions it came with.

3. Adjust the ball valve to get the flow of water you need.

4. Ensure that there are no leaks and make corrections if needed.

Stock and testing your system:

1. Add seedlings of your choosing to the grow bed.

2. Add a few fish to the tank.

3. Test the water twice a day, morning and evening, using an aquarium kit.

4. Test the pH levels and keep a log. Record the results and the quality of the water.

5. Now that you're up and running, all that's left to do is to feed the fish and get ready to harvest your vegetables.

Starting a Business Using Aquaponics

This type of agriculture has been around for a while now. There is a global demand for the aquaponics market. Many people are attracted to it because it presents a solution to the problems society faces in terms of food production and quality. Organic food is in high demand these days, and because the population is increasing and farmland is in short supply, aquaponics is becoming very profitable. Aquaponics is sustainable and eco-friendly and has made producing food efficient and low-cost. Aquaponics is not only for the backyard gardener, but it is being used for commercial purposes to meet the demand for organic food.

Starting up a commercial aquaponics system can be challenging. However, because of its efficiency and low-cost maintenance, it can turn out to be very profitable. Fresh, organic food is harvested much quicker than traditional farming methods; therefore, aquaponics is a worthwhile investment. Like any other business venture, careful planning, a strong business plan, and a committed team are essential to building your business. Before starting your business, you need to consider your main reasons for starting a commercial aquaponic business. Focus on your business plan, get expert advice, and identify resources that will help develop your business. Also, look out for issues that may hinder the progress of your business. Ask yourself these questions: What are the experiences that will help me with the farming operations? Will this business be for-profit and income? Do I have a location to run this from? What are the environmental issues that may crop up? Who on my team can help with business and financial strategies?

Your business plan should look something like this:

<u>Overview of your business:</u> Have a vision statement, a mission statement, and the goals for your business.

<u>Vision:</u> State the purpose of the business plan and prove you have an understanding of what is contained in the plan. Describe your vision for the commercial aquaponics farm and how it will tie into your personal beliefs and values. It should answer questions on community and environmental issues as well as how the farm will benefit the community.

<u>Mission:</u> These principles will guide you to the goal of your commercial aquaponics farm. It should also state the purpose and expectations of the farm and its customers.

<u>Goals:</u> Set short-term and long-term goals for the farm. Focus on the start-up process and extend your goals forward in time to what you would like the farm to achieve in the long-term.

<u>Management and Organization:</u> Set out the management and organization structure of the commercial aquaponics farm. How will the farm be managed and organized? Register your farm according to the legal requirements of the business; non-profit, sole proprietorship, or corporation. You may need to check the local and state requirements. Carefully set out the management team structure, including who will

manage and run the farm, what will their skills and responsibilities be, how will managers and board members be paid, how will the farm be managed and run?

Marketing Strategy: Identify your products and marketing strategies. The most important part of a business plan is to have a specific strategy for the sales and marketing of your product. Understanding the market is key, who are your potential customers and competitors? You have to believe in your product to convince potential investors that this is a viable market. Your business plan should include an introduction to your commercial aquaponics farm. These products will be produced and then sold, as well as how you plan on distributing the products, making them available to the consumers.

Identify your target market and their purchasing and spending rate. Gain an understanding of the location where your farm will be situated, will inflation or the employment rate affect you? What are the cultural and social factors that will affect your farm? Take into consideration your customers' values and behaviors. Do they have a preference for a specific crop? Ensure that your produce is readily available to the consumers so that they are more likely to buy from you. Ensure that the product meets the consumer's expectations by handling the crops with care from the time they've harvested to the time they are on the shelves. How will you be storing the product before distribution to ensure that the produce is fresh and of good quality?

With this information on hand, market your product as unique and different from the competitor's product. Note that your pricing must be comparable to your competitors. Take into consideration how you will dispose of products that are not sold. Identify your competitors and consider how you plan on competing with them. List your commercial aquaponic farm's advantages over the competitors as well as the disadvantages. Include what they offer to the market, their pricing, and how established they are in the area.

Operating Strategy: After you've identified the type of products and the quantity you would like to produce, prepare your operating strategy. List the methods you plan to use, such as the raft system, a nutrient film-based system, or a media-based system. What approach will you be using to raise the fish and plants? Prepare and discuss a schedule from the initial planting to the harvesting of the product. What are the volumes of fish and plants that must be managed when they're harvested? Do you plan on selling the fish as a product of the farm, or will they be used only to provide nutrition to the plants? Do you plan on planting and harvesting throughout the year or will it be seasonal?

The plants and the fish are dependent on each other, so ensure that you have enough fish to provide adequate nutrition for the plants. Invest in a cycling system that will need the needs of your farm. You will need a plan to manage the water pH, temperatures, nitrates, and ammonia levels. A good monitoring system will be needed as this is very important when growing healthy fish and plants. When choosing these systems, you will need to know the size of the system you plan to have and the capacity of fish and plants it will hold. Approximate the amount of fish and plants that you plan on producing and what the estimates would be for about five years. Discuss repeated production and how you will make sure this is consistent for each of these years.

List the resources that you will need, such as equipment, land, buildings, and anything necessary to start your commercial aquaponics farm. Also include waste disposal and the water and electricity requirements to meet the needs of your farm. What are the other objectives that you aim to meet, and how will this impact the environment? Where will the farm be situated for the next five years, in your home, a building, or a greenhouse? Most often, commercial aquaponic farms are in a controlled environment. Do you intend to buy or lease the property? What additional equipment and supplies such as tools, vehicles, tanks, etc., will be needed for the next five years, and how will you acquire them? Don't forget about a communications system, for monitoring the system remotely as well as internet and phone lines. Before you start your commercial aquaponics farm, make sure that all the environmental assessments have been done on the property and that all known issues have been resolved.

<u>Human Resources:</u> Estimate the number of workers that will be needed to manage and operate the business in the first five years. Identify the number of daily tasks and the workers that will complete them and include management, administrative as well as farm laborers. Create positions and the number of workers that you will need for each position. How many will be full-time employees and how many will be hired on a part-time basis? Do you plan on engaging volunteers to work on the farm? Do you plan on having a training program for the staff? How will you pay the staff and what would you estimate the salaries for each position to be? How would you structure the working hours? Will you have benefits such as medical coverage? Will you be using a monitoring system to reduce labor or hiring additional workers for harvesting? Ensure

that you have all the necessary licenses and permits required to start your commercial aquaponics farm. You must consider the governmental regulations, planning, zoning, and building requirements set out by the state in which you plan on operating.

Financial Strategy: Estimate the expenses that will be needed to start your commercial aquaponics farm. Draw up a five-year projection and include all expenses like marketing, operating, and human resources. This should also include preparations, administrative, and start-up costs. What is your income prediction annually for the first five years? The income must include sales projections as well as any losses from unsellable products. Also, include any donations or other monetary resources expected. Include current fixed assets such as buildings, furniture, machinery, etc., and any assets you may purchase in the future. List all the potential sources of funding, how much you will need, and how you intend to get the funding. The funds should have an impact on the business plan, ensuring that you achieve your goal of starting your very own commercial aquaponics farm.

There will, however, be potential risks that need to be considered. There will be risks in production as there may be crop failures, there will be risks in marketing, and your competitors may reduce their prices. You need to identify these potential risks and minimize them as they will definitely have an impact on the success of your business plan. To run a successful commercial aquaponics business, you need to have some kind of business experience in this field, or you will have to hire someone who does. Good business understanding, knowledge, and experience can guarantee you success in your business, while focusing on profitability and the idea of a commercial aquaponics farm does not.

Invest in yourself by educating and training yourself. Gaining knowledge in how aquaponics works and the science behind it is paramount to a thriving business. Speak to other successful aquaponics farmers to learn how they operate their business. Have a look at their facilities to see how their daily operations run. The right advice from the right people is important for your farm's success.

Do your research on pricing so that you can be competitive. Be knowledgeable about market trends so that you know which products are in demand. It is always better to start small and then build your business up from there. You will be able to gain some knowledge of how the business works, because no matter how much research you do, you will only truly understand how the business works from experience. You will be able to adapt quickly with a smaller and more manageable aquaponics farm. Things can suddenly go wrong, and you will be able to fix the problems easily and more efficiently. Even though aquaponics has the potential of making a lot of money, it is not easy work. You have to have a love for it to enjoy this challenging and labor-intensive field. Approach this business with the right mindset, extensive planning, and knowledge, and you will be able to achieve a successful and profitable commercial aquaponics farm.

Chapter 8:
The Ultimate Slow Fashion Guide for Anyone

Sustainability is not only about the planet, it's also about people and profit. Sustainable fashion is a circular system where clothes, shoes, and accessories are produced with integrity. Where laborers are treated humanely, the earth's resources are taken into consideration, and brands don't have to cut corners to be successful. Products are designed to be versatile and durable. Making fashion sustainable is extremely important, as fashion is the second most polluting industry. Over 150 billion items of clothing are produced each year.

Sustainable Fashion, to Purchase or Upcycle?

Even though over 70% of consumers say that sustainable fashion is very important to them, the fashion industry's efforts are slowing down. The fashion industry's interest varies, while some are conscious about choosing sustainable textiles, others prioritize labor practices. Here are three sustainable fashion categories:

1. **Rent instead of buying** - You can lease items of clothing, return them when you no longer need them and exchange them for something new.

2. **Resale and consignment** - Clothes can find multiple closets instead of ending up in a landfill. Loads of new people can use them. Thrift stores are an ever-popular place to buy second-hand clothes, and now you can thrift using Wi-Fi on a site called ThredUp. There are more than 35,000 brands to choose from, with up to 90% off. According to the calculations done by ThredUp, if everyone bought one used item instead of a brand new one in a year, 25 billion gallons of water and 449 million pounds of waste would be saved.

3. **Using recycled materials to create something new** - We've all heard that one person's trash is another person's treasure. Garments should ideally be passed down instead of being thrown away. Swap clothes for as long as possible, then use them for quilting projects or as rags. Canyon, an all-terrain sneaker brand, makes shoes entirely from recycled plastic bottles. Every pair uses 3.5 plastic bottles.

Upcycling waste is creative and challenging. Previously upcycling meant turning a pair of old jeans into a skirt, and these days, it's transforming clothes into something edgy, reinvigorating them with new life. The difference between recycling and upcycling is this, recycling is turning an old unused shirt into cleaning rags and upcycling is repurposing them into a one of a kind scarf. People have overflowing closets and they are left with the option of either disposing of or recycling their old clothing. Some people also have an attachment to clothing worn by deceased family members and have a hard time letting go of it. They can redesign and repurpose it to make something new and wear their loved one's clothes.

Another good way to reuse your outfits is to redesign them. Usually, the style of the garment becomes unfashionable, but the fabric does not. Upcycling seems to be a new movement in haute couture and everyone from the rich to young entrepreneurs is getting involved. Upcycling lessens the production of waste which would take thousands of years to break down, it preserves our natural resources and stops pollution, it saves you money by reinventing your old clothes, it preserves your parents' and grandparents' hand-me-downs, and it gives you a customized piece of clothing for yourself. If you keep old clothes long enough, they'll come back as retro fashion.

Fashion trends happen so quickly that there is always unused fabric lying around that can be used in hundreds of ways. Upcycling is a way for textile manufacturers to reuse their waste into something fashionable. It can be turned into paper pulp, rags, or even new garments. While some larger brands have adopted sustainable fashion practices, some have adopted the sustainable concept more as a marketing tool than to actually add value. There is a big difference between using sustainability for marketing and for building a company based on the concept. Contact the store directly if you're not sure whether they are a sustainable business or not. Ask the staff. Cotton and synthetics are harsher on the environment than linen or hemp because the pesticides and insecticides used to grow cotton are dangerous to the environment and to the farmers. Take note of the packaging, an environmentally conscious company will not use bubble wrap or plastic bags. Buy local garments, as they will travel a smaller distance using less energy.

Unfortunately, women between the ages of 25 and 35 reported that they were less concerned with environmental issues than the style and price of their clothes. They also wanted to know where these clothes had come from and who had worn them last. They voiced concerns about hygiene related to upcycled garments as well as the slightly higher price. These are concerns that you will have to contend with if you intend to sell upcycled clothing. Specifically, you will be up against the fast fashion industry.

Twenty items of clothing are manufactured for every person each year. This makes fashion a multi-trillion dollar industry. Fast fashion has fed this industry by making cheap clothes with a very low price tag. The fast fashion ideology shortens fashion cycles and decreases the customers' waiting period. This has increased the number of fashion seasons from 2 major seasons to approximately 100 micro-seasons. Because of this trend, customers are buying around 60% more but keeping the clothes for half the time. This has a tremendous impact on the environment.

Cotton is used 33% more than any other fiber and requires 2,700 liters of water to make a cotton shirt. This is what an average person drinks in 2 ½ years. The clothing industry is projected to skyrocket within the next few years, as an estimated 5.2 billion people enter middle-class lifestyles. While some will adopt new innovative ways that work to be sustainable, many others will be unlikely to change their traditional way of manufacturing. Clothing manufacturers must begin the transformation towards eradicating environmental risks. Companies must first recognize that they are expected to do more than just improve efficiency; they have to manufacture fewer, more durable products.

Selling Your Used Clothing

Are you ready to sell some clothes? How many items of clothing do you have that you are not using anymore? Pants, shoes, belts, and dresses, you probably have plenty of these, and it's time for them to have a brand new home. You can sell your unwanted clothes online if you're willing to put in a bit of work. You can make extra money quickly this way, potentially up to $1,000. Clothes that are fashionable and cute are always in demand, and it's never been easier to sell them. Besides making money, selling your unused clothing can help you organize your life by scaling down and your mornings less stressful, essentially decluttering your life. You can build a sustainable business from selling unwanted or barely used clothes. Here is a list of sites to help you find your fit and that can help you sell your unwanted items of clothing.

1. **ThredUp** - It's so simple, you can order a clean out kit from their site, put all the clothes you want to sell in the bags they

supply, and ship it back to them for free. Their second-hand experts will go through what you've sent them. They will take what they want and recycle the rest. It takes a few weeks before they get back to you with the price, and you can either donate it to a charity or get paid via PayPal. This is an effortless way to sell your clothes without negotiating or taking pictures of your items. ThredUp accepts high-quality women's and children's clothes that are still in good condition.

2. **Poshmark** - This is another easy site to use and is a great place to sell your clothes online. You will need to download the app, take some photos, and then share them. They will take a 20% fee, but for that percentage, you'll get no-hassle shipping. You can sell your clothes quickly, and you can negotiate the price.

3. **eBay** - You can probably sell your clothes on eBay for a lot more money than anywhere else. This site is excellent for rare items and high-end designers. Their fees are also much cheaper than other websites. You have the option to fix the price or auction them off.

4. **Depop** - This app is a bit like eBay and Instagram. It's aimed at teenagers and people in their 20s. Make sure you take great photos and have an excellent description. You can sell anything from vintage to quirky and unique items. Depop charges 10% on your sales, and they pay you via PayPal.

5. **Facebook Marketplace** - This is another great site for selling used clothing. Use your Facebook account, go to the marketplace icon, list your items, and click on and sell something. You can use this to sell to people in your area. Facebook Marketplace doesn't charge you for your use of their app, so you get to keep all the profits.

6. **Tradesy** - This is perfect if you have more than just clothes to sell. Handbags, accessories, or just about anything will make you some money here. Just make sure that they're all in good condition. They do charge a commission on your sales.

7. **Vinted** - This site is easy to use and is excellent for buyers and sellers. Once you've created an account, you will be able to list all the items you have for free. They

have great extra features as well. This is a great way to declutter your closet.

8. **Instagram** - This is perfect for girls who know how social media works, especially those that have a following. You can list your photos for free and you have control over pricing and marketing.

9. **Craigslist** - While this may not be trendy, it is an option. It is reliable and free, so you get to keep all the profits.

10. **Mercari** - This app has been designed to sell anything. It is user friendly and will cost you 10% of your sales.

11. **Rebag** - You can sell your designer handbags on this site. Your handbag must have a brand name on it for it to be considered. Send a photo of your bag, or you can visit them in the store for an assessment. They are quite strict, so check their requirements first. You'll receive a quote if your handbag has been approved.

12. **LePrix** - This is a great site if you have high-end designer items that are in excellent condition. You will be required to go through the authentication process first.

13. **The Real Real** - They work with brands like Prada, Gucci, Louis Vuitton, etc. High-end designer and fashion items. Send your items to them, and they will authenticate, price, and sell your items.

14. **Grailed** - They specialize in men's clothing, which makes it a great place to sell clothes and declutter your closet if you are a man.

15. **VarageSale** - Basically an old fashioned garage sale. You can sell anything and everything here. This app helps you sell in your local area, so there are no shipping fees to worry about. It's easy to use, just post a photo and description of the item and wait for the potential buyer to contact you. VarageSale checks out both buyers and sellers, so it is much safer than Craigslist and it's free.

16. **Material World** - This site works exactly like ThredUp.

You have a list of sites that you can use, but now you need some tips on how to be successful in selling your clothes. Check the clothes in your closet to see what you can sell. Remember, a lot of these sites are quite popular and can become crowded, so you need to stand out from the competition. Here are some easy tips and tricks to get the most out of selling your second-hand clothes.

1. Make sure that the item is worth selling. Take a look at items for sale that are similar to yours to see what people are prepared to pay. Make sure that your price is competitive. You may think that you will get close to what you paid for it, but that's highly unlikely. Before setting a price, take into consideration the work involved before you list. Don't set your price too low because it may not be worth it.

2. Prepare your clothes by giving them a makeover. Wash and iron them because they've probably been in your closet for a while now.

3. Prepare the stage for sales. People buy with their eyes, so make sure that you use an uncluttered background when you take a photo. Give them an Instagram look by photographing them on a flat surface and always use natural light. Brighten and crop the picture so that it looks exactly like the real item. A wooden hanger will make your clothes look smart.

4. Take photos that will sell your item. Think about what you would look for if you were to buy second-hand clothes online. Take a

few photos, at least one front, one back, and a close-up.

5. Add an accurate description and include the brand and the size of the item. Add some personal touches and give your opinion of the item and why you are selling it.

6. Make sure that you are selling your item when it is trendy and seasonal. No one will buy a swimsuit in the middle of winter.

7. Respond to the customer as soon as possible or straight away if you can. No one likes to wait, and you don't want them to move on to something else.

8. Work your shipping costs into the price. Get estimates for shipping and packaging in advance.

9. Most online apps charge their own fees. Consider this as well, as it will impact your profits.

10. Sell multiple items at once and save yourself some time. Do all steps from 1 - 10 for each item in your batch before uploading your items for sale. You'll sell more items more quickly this way.

With every new season, we're all planning on updating our wardrobes. We are usually running out of closet space and most importantly, money. Many of us suffer from buyer's remorse, so we all probably have clothes that still have the tags on or clothes that we thought were a great buy at the time but turned out to be not so great. You might as well make some money and get rid of some of those unwanted fashion faux pas. Treat yourself and your closet to a fresh new look. You'll be surprised at how many people will pay for the clothes you no longer need.

With the endless online possibilities for selling your clothes, please be aware that there are people out there ready to scam you. Read all the fine print and the site's policies before you commit yourself. If you find that it's just too much work to photograph the clothes before selling them online, then a consignment store is the option for you. Most consignment stores work the same, you take your clothes in, they make you an offer, and you can either accept or decline. A Google search for consignment stores in your area will be a good start. Some popular shops are Clothes Mentor and Plato's Closet. Of course, you can also consider ThredUp, which we mentioned above.

You're probably not going to be getting rich quickly by this method unless you want to dip your hand into the million-dollar second hand and used item businesses. However, try not to give up if your first sales turn out to be difficult. Use this as a learning process and get a system in place. Many people do this, and as long as you don't become discouraged, it can be fun and rewarding.

Chapter 9:
Selling Used Books

Would you like to do your part for sustainable reading and help the environment? Readers know the value of knowledge; we love our books because they allow us to transform ourselves through education. There is something magical about books. We can catch a glimpse into the world around us through our imagination. Our love for books, especially the ones in print form, could be damaging the environment. As responsible citizens, we have to do the right thing.

Over two billion books are printed in the USA each year, and that means about 30 million trees are destroyed. That's enough trees to fill 37,000 football fields, which is equivalent to the size of Washington DC. The manufacturing of paper uses lots of oil and gas; in fact, the world's third-largest user of fossil fuels is the paper industry. Most of the time, books are not read and then passed on to someone else to read and enjoy. Although it would be great if they were, the truth is that over 10 million trees' worth of books ends up destroyed.

When a book is released, thousands of copies are printed at once to bring down the printing cost. In many cases, most of these books are not sold, so they end up being destroyed. They could even be left in a warehouse, never to be used, or remaindered. Remaindered refers to books that have been sold to a discount book store that sells former best-sellers at a discounted price. There are, however, books that made their way to a bookstore but were not sold. Now, bookstores can ask the publisher for a refund, but because of high shipping costs, the bookstore tears off the cover of the book and sends it back alone, leaving the entire book unsellable. These books are pulped, meaning they're recycled into paper. The recycling process isn't very eco-friendly because it takes a lot of electricity and chemicals to break down the paper before it can be used for other products. Each year, 16,000 truckloads of unread books are destroyed. We need to make books more environmentally friendly.

Sustainable Reading

Digital reading is the easiest way to foster sustainable reading and stop the destructive cycle of trees. Even though digital reading devices such as iPads, Kindles, and e-readers do leave a carbon footprint, they have a much lower impact on the environment. We must commit to reduce our carbon footprint and be good stewards of the earth and the environment. These days, you don't even need a Kindle to read on because you can use your phone or laptop. Reading 100 books on your Kindle or phone is far more environmentally friendly than reading those books in print. So as an avid reader, switching to e-books can help the environment.

If you're not a fan of e-books and must have a book to hold and pages to turn, look for sustainable print options. Visit your local library, as this is the most sustainable option. Books that have been lent out over and over again maximize the utility of the resources that go into publishing a book. Build your collection of used books if you don't want to borrow from the library. You can buy used books from online used booksellers or even your local bookstore. Some bookshops offer a buy-back system, which means you will get store credit when you return your used book. You can do your part by donating the books you've read to a charity where they will be reread.

Another sustainable publishing option is print on demand. The POD system prints only the books that have been sold, so a book is printed only when a customer places an order for it. It is then packed and shipped directly to the customer. POD suppliers ensure that they use at least 30% recycled paper when they print their books.

What Types of Books Can You Sell?

If you're looking for a way to make some money on the weekend, then this is for you. Turn your old books into profit. Books have become one of the top-selling online categories, and some publishing companies have even reported higher sales from online sources than from their physical outlets. If you're an entrepreneur who wants to learn how to sell online or someone who has tons of used books that you'd like to rehome, this chapter will guide you into the online book sales business. One of the keys to buying and selling books online is to know how much people are willing to pay for them before you sell them. Just because you can buy a book for $1 does not mean that you should. Only buy a book if you know for sure that you can make some money on it. If you're wondering which books would make you the most money, well, it will depend on what is in demand and how your business is promoted. The four types of books that are usually needed are:

Textbooks - This market is estimated at between $5 billion and $8.5 billion. There is a lot of money that can be made from this. Even though many textbooks are sold on campus, many people still buy and sell them online. If you want to sell your textbooks, that's great, but why not become a "textbook flipper" by buying them and reselling them for a profit? You can start looking at places like garage sales and second-hand stores and ask your family and friends. You might be lucky and find one or two on eBay, Amazon, or even Craigslist. You can sell textbooks almost anywhere, and eBay and Amazon are great online sites that you can list your books on. Other marketplaces are textbook specific. Take a look at the following list: Textbooks.com, BookScouter.com, Chegg.com, CampusBookRentals.com, and AbeBooks.

Modern First Edition Books - These are books that were published in the last 30 or 40 years. They are collectibles for some people, who enjoy these books and authors, and for others, they will pay a higher price for something that may become collectible in the future. Recent first editions are relatively easy to find, as it's the first editions printed many years ago that tend to be rare. The older the first edition is, the higher the profit for you. To determine whether the book is the first edition or not, check for some of these:

1. First Edition or First Published will appear on the copyright page.

2. A number line is present, 987654321, if a 1 is present, this will be the first edition. For the second printing, the 1 will be removed, and the lowest number will be 2.

3. The date appears on both the title page and the copyright page.

eBay is a great place to sell your modern first edition books.

Out of Print Used Books - These are your regular run of the mill books. There's not too much money in them. You will be able to find them in any bookshop or thrift store.

Collectible and Antique Books - You can use a book scanner app, which will give you the potential profit margin for a book, especially if you're selling on a marketplace.

How to Promote and Sell Your Books

In order for you to sell books online, you need to set up an independent bookstore. This way, you will maximize profits without having to pay out commission on your sales. Shopify is ideal, and it supports a wide range of templates. Shopify works great on mobile devices, giving you the opportunity to sell to mobile shoppers. Some legalities must be taken care of when starting an online business. You must register your business's name and get a tax number, as you don't want complications later on. You can be fined for running a business without registration. You will also need to register a domain name for your bookstore.

Once you've done all that, the next step is to promote your bookstore and expose your brand. A marketing strategy is beneficial to any entrepreneur, as you can send potential customers a newsletter and links to your products. Upload good quality images of your products, run competitions, and share discount coupons. Connections with social media influencers will give you an added advantage, as you can get them to review a book or share your store link on their platforms. Social media influencers can be found on Facebook, Instagram and YouTube. Keep up your momentum when you're promoting your bookstore. After Google, YouTube is the second biggest search engine in the world. So posting a detailed video about your bookstore on YouTube is a great way to generate interest. The next step would be to find a wholesale book supplier. Buying stock at a wholesale price will give you a good margin, and you will be able to get discounts from them after a while. You can get all genres of books from these suppliers:

1. **Used Wholesale Books** - They have about 7 million books for sale at any time. They also have a wide variety of wholesale, fiction and kids books, which are in excellent condition to buy.

2. **Bulk Bookstore** - They offer up to 55% discounts with free shipping. Use their online catalog to check the availability of books or you can send them your list to get a quote. You can get anything from first edition books to textbooks from Bulk Bookstore.

3. **Book Depot** - They offer books for 75% - 90% off the list price. Their books are genuine and in excellent condition. The book categories range from philosophy to antiques, from games to medical. Blow out books are sold at a fraction of the cost, and if you don't mind dusting, it can help you save even more money.

4. **Better World Books** - They offer media stock and bulk books ranging from religious texts to best sellers. They have a large variety of leather-bound and vintage books. Books are sold by a box, a pallet, or a container so the price will depend on what you're buying.

You can find amazing books at yard sales and offline distributors as well. You could buy stock for 10¢ a book this way. Craigslist and eBay have first edition books as well as textbooks for sale. All of these options will allow you to get books that you can resell on another marketplace for a profit.

Of course, you can resell your books on Amazon, eBay, or Craigslist, which we have discussed in previous chapters. However, there are many other websites and brick and mortar stores that you can use to sell your books. Here are the 5 best places to sell hardcovers, paperbacks, and textbooks:

1. **Half Price Books** - This is the USA's biggest family-owned bookstore, with over 120 stores. Take your books to one of their outlets to get an appraisal, and Half Priced Books will make you an offer.

2. **Book Scouter.com** - You will be able to get a good idea as to what different companies are willing to pay for your books. Prices always change, so don't wait too long to make the sale.

3. **AbeBooks Buyback** - Consider using this service to sell your textbooks. They will beat the price of the local college bookstore. Don't send them damaged books because they will be recycled and you won't get anything out of it.

4. **Powell's Books** - You can take your books to one of their stores or use their website, get an appraisal, and sell your

books. They work similarly to Half Price Books. The books must be in pristine condition before they take them. Check their website to learn what issues would make them reject a book. However, Powell's will give you a store credit if they take your books.

5. **Textbooks.com** - This company not only buys used textbooks, but they also sell them to students and guarantee them cashback on certain books. You can sell all your college textbooks on this site.

You will need a solid knowledge of self-publishing if you've written a few books and would like to sell them online. Some platforms can help you with this, one such example is:

Blurb - Writers learn how to sell their books in various formats online. You can create, promote, and publish your book. You will also be able to change your book into a photo book, trade book, magazine, e-books, etc. Blurb will handle shipping for you. Pick a template and upload your book, it's that easy. Blurb's Adobe InDesign allows you to build your own template, but there are loads of templates to complement any industry. Now that your book is ready, go to "Sell and Distribute" and set the price. Get the word out about your book, market and promote it on all social media platforms. Hand out free copies and ask for reviews. Blurb will send you a payment on any sales at the end of the month.

Amazon - You can design your books using a third-party website and sell your books here on Amazon. Give Amazon your ISBN and your book will be ready for self-publishing. After you've set up your author profile, you can set the price of the book. Amazon does charge a fee to prepare the book, so add this to your price. If you're selling third party books, this is relatively easy to do, send the stock to Amazon and they will take care of the shipping and handling for you.

Tips for First-Timers

Here are some tips if you're selling books for the first time. List your books properly and be transparent about the condition of the books. Mention whether there are missing pages, highlighted passages, or any writing in the books. If you're not upfront about the condition of the book, the buyer may reject your book altogether. But if you are honest, they know what to expect and will probably just decrease their offer or only make an offer if they don't mind the condition. You'll get positive feedback and make loads of money.

If your books are in great condition, make sure that you package them carefully before shipping them off. It is your responsibility to make sure that the books arrive in one piece and without damage, otherwise you are likely to end up with negative reviews and refund requests. You can save yourself some cash by getting the buyer to pay for shipping. If you're considering selling old or used magazines, this is a tricky one, as you may not make any money for the effort you'll put in. You're actually better off just donating them to a retirement home or recycling them.

Another useful tip is to download the bookscouter.com app. If you have books to sell and you're not sure what the going rate is for them, this will be your saving grace. Just enter the ISBN into the app, and it will show what people are willing to pay for the book. Download the free mobile app, which will be quite handy when you're browsing through thrift stores or yard and estate sales. You will be able to enter the ISBN to see the current selling price, so you don't miss an opportunity to make a good profit.

The end... almost!

Reviews are not easy to come by.

As an independent author with a tiny marketing budget, I rely on readers, like you, to leave a short review on Amazon.

Even if it's just a sentence or two!

So if you enjoyed the book, please...

leave a brief review on Amazon.

I am very appreciative for your review as it truly makes a difference.

Thank you from the bottom of my heart for purchasing this book and reading it to the end.

Chapter 10:
Candle Making

Candle making is a wonderful world of beauty and color. One where you make money and have some fun while doing it. In medieval times, chandlery, or candle making, was actually a rather masculine skill. Everyone relied on candles then, from businesses to homes and churches. Candles were made from wax or tallow, which is the fat from cows and sheep. It was a rather lucrative profession then as light was a necessity to all kingdoms and villages. Candles may be simple, but they are hugely significant. They were a luxury item given as gifts during festivals. Candles were also used in spiritual worship, with many different cultures using their own methods and products. The Qin dynasty used beeswax and whale fat for their candles. Candles in India were made with cinnamon and yak butter, which were the world's first scented candles. The indigenous people of North America used candlefish or smelt fish as a source of lighting. This was great for sustained light but had a very unpleasant odor. The first commercial candle makers were born after the fall of the Roman Empire when there was a shortage of oil for oil lamps. Once the lightbulb was invented, the need for candles dwindled.

However, the popularity of candles has grown in recent years. Although candles aren't a necessity, they do add a romantic ambiance to any room. Depending on what you're going for, candles have lovely scents like sandalwood and bourbon. Homemade candles cost a fraction of a store-bought one, and they burn and smell just as good as the expensive kind. This natural process won't take you more than a few hours and will make great gifts for friends and family. There are loads of different types of candles out there, but the easiest one for a beginner is a container candle. These are candles that come in mason jars or containers, and the best part is you don't need specialized tools or equipment to make them. In this chapter, you will find not only inspiration but also actionable steps to embark on your very own candle making journey. This chapter covers everything you need to know, from the tools that you need to add your own personal touches to the candles.

You can start your very own candle making business with just a few easy steps. You will need to decide what type of candle you would like to make and what recipe will work best. There is a difference between making and creating, and the goal is to create natural and organic candles. For you to create, you must understand how each ingredient reacts to each other and how they interact. To make your business successful, your product must stand out; it must be unique. Lots of local stores sell candles, so you won't have a business if you're making carbon copies.

However, you can look at the candle industry for inspiration. Look at what types of candles are being produced already. Candlemakers and perfumers have joined forces to give us luxury fragrant candles. Other companies are embedding small prizes in their candles, with a small chance to win something valuable. These candles can cost you anything from $50 or more. You may be interested in making something like this, or you may identify a missing niche in the market. Maybe there is a smell combination you would like that isn't readily available, or perhaps you have a particular candle aesthetic in mind.

Many people love the effect of the warm glow that the candles give off, making their homes cozy and comfortable. Soy candle making is another inexpensive method that leaves ample room for your creativity to run free. You can buy supplies for a dozen homemade candles for the cost of a few store-bought ones. It's so easy once you get started. However, it can get complicated at the same time. You can make a few candles within an hour with a few supplies, but getting the perfect result can be a bit tricky. We will go over a summary of the candle-making process and give more detailed options and recipes. Over time you will be able to tweak and adjust the recipe to suit your needs and even come up with your very own unique blends of fragrances.

When making your candles, be creative in choosing a candle container, use mason jars, drinking glasses, mugs, tins, ceramic flower pots, teacups, or even small bowls. Just make sure that they are heat safe. To determine how much wax you will need for your chosen container, fill it with water, then pour it into a measuring cup. This way, you won't waste any wax. Next, choose the wick size. Then weigh in the correct amount of wax on the scale. For every 1 ounce of fluid, you will need 1 ounce in weight of wax. Weighing out the fragrances can be tricky because the properties vary one from the other. Basically, you will need 1 ounce of fragrance per 1 pound wax. You can adjust this as you go if you're not satisfied with the scent.

Getting Started

Let's talk about the supplies and tools you will need to get started and then go over the steps in more detail. Because the startup cost for candle making is quite low, you will be creating several candles with only a few supplies and tools.

You will need the following supplies:

- Heat-proof jars and other candle containers

- Pre-waxed and pre-tabbed wicks

- Soy wax flakes or any other wax of your choice

- Superglue

- A double boiler or a large pot to use as a double boiler

- Melting pot, large glass, heat-proof pitcher, or bowl

- Wooden mixing spoon or spatula

- Scale

- Thermometer

- Masking tape or old pens

- Fragrant essential oils

- Paper towels

Wax: This the primary ingredient of any candle. There are three types of candle making wax for you to choose from:

- **Paraffin:** This has been used for hundreds of years; it's cheap and can be easily colored and scented. This traditional wax is petroleum-based and toxic, so you should get an all-natural alternative product.

- **Soy:** This is new on the market and is quickly becoming popular. It is made with soybean oil but is sometimes blended with paraffin, palm wax, or beeswax. You can also add color and scent to soy wax.

- **Beeswax:** Bees produce this as a byproduct of honey making. This is entirely natural and gold in color, with a slight sweet scent to it. Beeswax is considered the oldest ingredient in candle making; some of these candles were found in the pyramids. However, you won't be able to add to its scent and it is quite expensive.

Waxes for candle making usually come in small pellet forms, which makes it easier to melt. If the wax does come in large blocks, cut it into small manageable pieces. A must for candle making is a double boiler or large pot in which you can melt your wax. There are hundreds of fragrant oils to choose from and use. You can choose from essential oils or fragrances specially formulated for use in candle making. Candlescience.com has scents such as Fireside, Buttered Rum, Whiskey and Apples, and Maple Bourbon. The wicks are also an important part of the candle. Wicks are sized, small, medium, and large. The length does not matter as you can trim it to your desired length.

Get some containers: mugs, mason jars, shot glasses, or anything else that can be used to house a candle. Just make sure they can withstand the heat of a lighted candle. Another tool you should have is a thermometer because fragrances are added when the wax reaches a specific temperature. You will also need a spatula or spoon to stir the wax. The process for all wax types is roughly the same. Now we can move on to the really exciting part of making our very own candle in a container. Remember, safety first! You will be working with very hot wax.

Step 1. Prepare the work area.

Be prepared for the wax to get on everything, and you will probably only find out where once it's dry. Use old newspapers or paper towels to cover the work area. It's a quick process once you get started, so have everything you need close at hand.

Step 2. Melt the wax.

Melt the wax in a double boiler. It usually takes about 10 - 15 minutes to melt. Use the spatula to stir or break up the bigger chunks. The ideal temperature can vary by wax type and ranges from 120 to 180 degrees Fahrenheit. It is best to check the information for the specific wax you purchase.

Step 3: Adhere the wick to the container.

Some wicks come with a built-in sticker that you can use to stick to the bottom of your container. However, most don't, so you can use superglue or the old candle makers trick of dipping the metal tab into the liquid wax and quickly sticking it into the center of the container. The wax will harden after a few minutes, and the wick will be stuck to the bottom.

Step 4: Add fragrant oils.

Once the wax has melted until liquid, add your preferred scent to the double boiler. The temperature can also vary by wax type for this step. In the case of soy wax, add fragrance at 175 to 185 degrees Fahrenheit. Stir to distribute the fragrance. Different types of wax require different amounts of fragrance, so take note of the instructions that come with the wax.

Step 5: Pour into the container.

When the scented wax has cooled to about 130 - 140 degrees Fahrenheit, pour it into your preferred container. Lightly hold on to the wick so that it doesn't move. Leave a little wax in the double boiler for later.

Step 6. Secure the wick.

The wick may move around in the wax and could harden off-center. To ensure that this does not happen use some old pens and secure the wick between them on top of the container. Once the wick is secure, you can remove the pens. If the wick is off-center, it won't burn properly.

Step 7. Cool and top off.

Once the wax cools and settles, you may find that a sinkhole has formed in the middle. Reheat the leftover wax and fill in the hole. Add enough just to fill in the depression and for a smooth finish. Too much wax may cause another sinkhole to form.

Step 9. Trim the wick.

Trim the wick to about a ¼ of an inch. If the wick is too long, it will burn too hot and too big.

Step 10. Clean up.

The easiest way to clean up any wax that has spilled is to wipe it up while it's still in liquid form. If it does harden, you can easily scrape the wax off the surface of your tools, countertops, etc. You can then wash normally.

Things to remember:

Allow the candles to cool for at least 24 hours before lighting them. Ensure that the surface that the candle is on is stable. Keep the candles away from children and pets. Never leave a burning candle near anything combustible or unattended. It may take some time to get the desired scent or for it to be perfectly smooth. Take heart that with every batch of candles you make, you're one step closer to perfection.

How to Start Selling Your Homemade Candles Online

Homemade candles are in much higher demand than mass-produced ones. They're easy to sell and cheaper to make. What better reasons could there be for you to sell them online and from home? Selling candles online will be your entry into the world of e-commerce and running a successful online business from home. You can build a strong marketing strategy with some interesting facts about the candle industry.

Also, consider the reasons people would purchase a candle when designing your business. People usually buy candles as home decor elements, to reduce stress, and for aromatherapy. They use candles to make their homes cozy and comfortable, usually placing them in bedrooms and living rooms, sometimes even in their bathrooms. The fragrance and how the candles look influences customers' purchasing decisions. Candles make great gifts for birthdays, housewarmings, and thank you gifts. Men and women both appreciate candles as gifts, making candles quite a popular item.

With that in mind, you want to ensure that there is a market for what you're selling. Do market research to determine which of the below candle components you can use and categories you can target to maximize your sales.

Scented or Aromatherapy Candles - These are used to bring a fragrant smell to their homes. They are bought for special occasions. There is a wide variety of scents that you can use:

- Vanilla and nutmeg
- Mandarine
- Sandalwood
- Tobacco
- Lavender
- Peach

The list goes on and on. Aromatherapy candles have hints of essential oil that help soothe the mind and the body. You can buy all you need from Amazon or from your local supply store.

Coloring - Each coloring has its pros and cons, and there are many types that you can add to your candles. Listed here a few choices as well as how well they work:

a) Color Blocks - These provide the richest color and are by far the cheapest option to color your candles. Even though they are very cost-effective, it is difficult to get the precise color you want every single time. Try using color blocks for dark-colored candles only.

b) Liquid Dyes - These are absolutely perfect for achieving the shade of color you are looking for. However, all liquid dyes have a hint of a chemical smell.

c) Color Chips - These are slightly overpriced and you may have a problem with achieving the color you're looking for. Give it a go and see if you like it.

d) Crayons - If you're making a few candles to try out the process, these can be a good option. They are, however, not something you should consider if you're making high-quality candles.

Candle Additives - Additives are used to enhance the quality of a candle. Many candle makers use this method, and although this is not recommended, you once again should decide whether this is a good option for you. Here is a list of additives:

a) Vybar - This is used to enhance the scent of the candle. It produces a marbled look on the top and gives the entire candle an opaque look. It will help you create a really nice looking candle.

b) UV Light Protectors - First off, these are expensive. UV light protectors ensure that the candle's natural color is maintained because otherwise, the color will fade if left for too long in the sun. This will be an excellent investment if you're planning on selling them wholesale.

c) Petrolatum - Add some of this to your wax if the wax you're using does not hold to the sides of your containers. Petrolatum will absorb more fragrance but will not burn cleanly. It should be noted that this is a petroleum byproduct and may not be desirable for eco-friendly candles.

d) Crisco Shortening - Believe it or not, Crisco shortening is great for a quality candle. It has several benefits, as it decreases wet spots and helps absorb the scent. However, some believe that the fumes from burning Crisco can be toxic, so it is up to you whether you would like to use it.

Selling Decorative Candles - When making decorative candles, how the candles look is most important. People buy these to decorate their rooms. They come in so many different shapes and colors. Search online to get an idea of what is in demand and for inspiration.

Soy and Vegan Candles - These are made from soybean extract and are in very high demand. They burn longer and cleanly. Soy candles sell for a higher price so you can give this one a go.

There are lots of other types of candles that you can make and sell. While you explore the opportunities to sell candles, always check whether they are in demand before you commit. You need something unique that will intrigue the online shoppers. Before you can start making candles, you must think about how you're going to sell them. You can sell your candles on popular marketplaces such as eBay, Amazon, or Etsy, but if you are serious about this, why not start your own online store? Alternatively, you can work on your website while selling on these marketplaces. It is important to establish your online presence and stand out if you want to do better than your competitors within the first year of your business. The process is straightforward, whether you want to make a bit of extra income or if you want a successful online business. However, getting your product noticed is the hard part.

Making candles and starting a website is pretty easy; the tricky part is marketing. So, what are the best marketing strategies to sell candles online? Whichever platform you plan on using to sell your candles online, you must first let your customers know about them. You can run a Facebook ad or make an Instagram account. This is the easiest and cheapest way to get your product noticed. These platforms have a massive audience for you to tap into. You don't have to wait until you have a finished product, start now. Add videos that show your progress and start a blog. This will generate interest in your business even before it gets off the ground. Include links to your products to increase traffic and most importantly, sales.

Candle making can be very profitable if you can make a great candle. Always continue to better your craft even if you start making money immediately. Have an effective distribution system, and try to get your candles into local stores as well. The demand for candles is steadily increasing, and that presents a wonderful opportunity for you to generate interest and demand for your product. Remember, any business can be a good business. The amount of sales you make is totally up to you.

Starting a candle making business is a perfect example of how you can turn your hobby into a moneymaker either full-time or part-time. One of the hottest topics around the world these days is "Going Green." "Green" is associated with products and or services that are effective in promoting environmental protection. The candle market is full of renewable raw materials. Many people are choosing green candles that use beeswax or soy wax, and both are eco-friendly. Glass candle containers are also considered green, as they can be recycled and reused. Your marketing strategy could look like this, the wax is a natural product, and the glassware is 100% recycled glass. This will appeal to everyone who is environmentally conscious. The wick is also a natural product, and it's 100% cotton. This type of marketing opens the doors to a rapidly growing segment of customers, and it helps out the planet!

Conclusion

I hope that you gained a better understanding of how our economy works as you've journeyed through this book. What is necessary to be successful and to have fulfillment? Many topics have been covered in this book, from economics to entrepreneurship. The many fundamental economic concepts we've explained hopefully no longer seem mysterious and will guide your decisions as you form your own business.

I do hope that this book has been an eye-opener in terms of how everyday economics works. It's hard to get people excited about economics and to get them to think about how economics can be applied in everyday life. Economics puts a theory behind our daily actions. Economics, in a nutshell, is how we, as consumers use the limited amount of resources we have available to maximize our satisfaction by buying the products we will find most useful. It deals with the consumption of these products, as well as how the products are priced. You now understand why price is important and how it can be used strategically.

There are also many subheadings and different categories that fall under the economics title. You can see how human behavior influences people's purchasing decisions and how entrepreneurs can use this information to inform their marketing decisions. It can make you think about why you pay what you do for your groceries, perhaps even understanding the part we all play in the price structures. We, the consumers, define economics, and we can use this in our business strategies to bring us favorable results. The psychology behind the pricing system and human behavior is something astounding. The aim of explaining this is so that you can go into your dream venture armed with a wealth of knowledge and insights that very few entrepreneurs have. An entrepreneur has rarely been formally educated in economic matters. They are creative and full of boundless energy ready to take on the world, the business world that is, without giving any thought to the inner workings of the economy.

The business world has been turned on its head during the last few years. Almost everyone from the layman to the world's richest man is constantly reminded that we are responsible for destroying our planet. We have to act and act fast if we want to preserve and restore our beautiful planet. Entrepreneurs again are at the forefront, with their new ways of thinking and their positive business principles, which make the rest of the business world sit up and take notice. They are pushing boundaries, yet remaining true to ethical and sustainable methods. Entrepreneurship is slowly shifting the business landscape. With new technologies released almost daily and with customers looking for niche markets, it can be challenging to keep up. New businesses must embrace the change and keep up to date with what is unique in the industry. Have an edge against your competitors and keep your business moving successfully forward.

The internet is a great place to start generating an additional or alternate income. Digital entrepreneurship is one way of starting your own business with a small amount of funds. Even though digital entrepreneurship requires quite a bit of time and effort in the beginning, the rewards make it worthwhile once it gains momentum. Hopefully, you will use the tips and advice given throughout this book to implement successful marketing strategies and avoid common mistakes. You will be able to make wiser decisions in your own company. There are hundreds and thousands of dollars to be made through genuine money-making opportunities. With hard work and through developing yourself, you will turn whatever you call a hobby into something extremely lucrative. Be eco-friendly and fashion-forward. Remember that repetition is no longer a sin, and you don't need to buy new clothes. Wasting should never be an option for anyone and any business. The business of selling used books online will work well for those who have a love for the written word, for those who love old and antique books, and for those who love going to estate and yard sales. You can turn that small business idea of yours into a sustainable source of additional income.

I sincerely hope that you have found inspiration in this book to become part of the change that the world needs. There is no better time than the present to change the world. To know that you can have a positive impact on our planet and to create an income stream is literally a dream come true for many. With many inspiring examples of successful people who have tried what you're about to try and have become successful, use these examples and the tried and tested strategies to create great sustainable products. Connect and network with like-minded business associates and potential customers and become part of this amazing movement.

Starting your own business is not as easy as it seems. However, the benefits far outweigh the effort and hard work it takes to launch your business. Remember that what you're building will give you a source of pride and achievement.

You will learn new and exciting skills, be independent, and follow your passion. You will be able to create more jobs and make lots of money.

Do what you love. Be patient, and don't give up even if the first results are discouraging. Learn how to make money and how to save money. Support the planet and your community. Live a healthy life and live the life you've always dreamed of.

References

1.1 What Is Economics, and Why Is It Important? – Principles of Economics. (2015). Opentextbc.Ca. https://opentextbc.ca/principlesofeconomics/chapter/1-1-what-is-economics-and-why-is-it-important/

1.2 Microeconomics and Macroeconomics – Principles of Economics. (2019). Opentextbc.Ca. https://opentextbc.ca/principlesofeconomics/chapter/1-2-microeconomics-and-macroeconomics/

5.3 Elasticity and Pricing – Principles of Economics. (2011). Opentextbc.Ca. https://opentextbc.ca/principlesofeconomics/chapter/5-3-elasticity-and-pricing/

6 Essential Behavioral Economics Principles for Business | Brandtrust. (2018, April 18). Brandtrust. http://brandtrust.com/behavioral-economics/

A beginners' guide to aquaponics. (2018, May 11). Thefishsite.Com.

https://thefishsite.com/articles/a-beginners-guide-to-aquaponics

A Complete Guide to Aquaponic Gardening. (2018). Green and Vibrant. https://www.greenandvibrant.com/aquaponic-gardening

Abadie, M.-J. (2020). The Everything Candlemaking Book: Create Homemade Candles in Housewarming Colors, Interesting Shapes, and Appealing Scents (Everything®) - Kindle edition by Abadie, Marie-Jeanne. Crafts, Hobbies & Home Kindle eBooks @ Amazon.com. Amazon.Com. https://www.amazon.com/Everything-Candlemaking-Book-House-Warming-Interesting-ebook/dp/B005I5EL2A/ref=sr_1_5?crid=2IPL57477MFTZ&dchild=1&keywords=candle+making&qid=1588487798&s=digital-text&sprefix=candle%2Cdigital-text%2C239&sr=1-5

Amadeo, K. (2020, February 15). Where's the Best Standard of Living? Depends Who You Ask. The Balance. https://www.thebalance.com/standard-of-living-3305758

Art. (2019a, May 14). How To Make Your Own Candles at Home | The Art of Manliness. The Art of Manliness. https://www.artofmanliness.com/articles/diy-chandlery-how-to-make-your-own-candles/

Balram, S. (2018, June 9). Reject, revamp, repeat! Why fashion upcycling is now an A-list pursuit. The Economic Times. https://economictimes.indiatimes.com/m agazines/panache/why-fashion-upcycling-is-now-an-a-list-pursuit/articleshow/64523807.cms?from =mdr

Basic Economic Lessons that Growth Entrepreneurs Should Heed. (2011, August 20). Edward Lowe Foundation. https://edwardlowe.org/basic-economic-lessons-that-growth-entrepreneurs-should-heed-2/

Baumann, K. (2011, October 18). What's the importance of price elasticity of demand to the government? | eNotes. ENotes. https://www.enotes.com/homework-help/whats-importance-price-elasticity-demand-285809

Bensonhoff, K. (2019, August 13). The Online Future of Entrepreneurship: A New Age.

Business 2 Community. https://www.business2community.com/st artups/the-online-future-of-entrepreneurship-a-new-age-02239805

Biddle, D. (1993, November). Recycling for Profit: The New Green Business Frontier. Harvard Business Review. https://hbr.org/1993/11/recycling-for-profit-the-new-green-business-frontier

Bratskeir, K. (2019, September 12). Your complete guide to sustainable fashion—the movement disrupting the industry. Ideas. https://www.wework.com/ideas/worklife/your-complete-guide-to-sustainable-fashion-the-movement-disrupting-the-industry

Brooke, N. (2020). Aquaponics for Beginners: How to Build your own Aquaponic Garden that will Grow Organic Vegetables - Kindle edition by Brooke, Nick. Crafts, Hobbies & Home Kindle eBooks @ Amazon.com. Amazon.Com. https://www.amazon.com/Aquaponics-Beginners-Aquaponic-Organic-Vegetables-ebook/dp/B07KXG7BQ6/ref=sr_1_8?dch ild=1&keywords=sustainable+money+ma

king&qid=1588427109&s=digital-text&sr=1-8

Burnett, G. (2018, March 1). Upcycling - An Absolute Beginner's Guide. Georgina Burnett. https://www.georginaburnett.com/upcycling-beginners-guide/

Chladek, N. (2019, November 6). The Importance of Business Sustainability Strategies | HBS Online. Business Insights - Blog. https://online.hbs.edu/blog/post/business-sustainability-strategies

Davis, R. (2020, January 19). Aquaponics System Design, Aquaponics DIY. Grow Food Guide. https://growfoodguide.com/aquaponics/what-is-the-best-aquaponics-system-design/

Dillehay, J. (2020). Start a Creative Recycling Side Hustle: 101 Ideas for Making Money from Sustainable Crafts Consumers Crave - Kindle edition by Dillehay, James. Arts & Photography Kindle eBooks @ Amazon.com. Amazon.Com. https://www.amazon.com/Start-Creative-Recycling-Side-Hustle-ebook/dp/B084DCPWKW/ref=sr_1_2?dc hild=1&keywords=sustainable+money+m

aking&qid=1588427109&s=digital-text&sr=1-2

Drew, D., & Yehounme, G. (2017). The Apparel Industry's Environmental Impact in 6 Graphics | World Resources Institute. Wri.Org. https://www.wri.org/blog/2017/07/appar el-industrys-environmental-impact-6-graphics

Firms in competitive markets - Baripedia. (n.d.). Baripedia.Org. Retrieved May 23, 2020, from https://baripedia.org/wiki/Firms_in_com petitive_markets

Green Candlemaking: Environmentally Friendly Options | Candlewic. (n.d.). Www.Candlewic.Com. Retrieved May 23, 2020, from https://www.candlewic.com/education/sh opping-help/green-candle-making/green-candlemaking-environmentally-friendly-options/page.aspx?id=1727

Hall, M. (2019). What Is Purchasing Power Parity—PPP? Investopedia. https://www.investopedia.com/updates/p urchasing-power-parity-ppp/

Hatchett, F. (2019, October 12). How to Sell Books Online and 5 Places to Sell Them!

Ecom Elites | Best Shopify & Drop Shipping Training Course! https://ecomelites.com/how-to-sell-books-online/

How profitable is a candle-making business? - Quora. (n.d.). Www.Quora.Com. Retrieved May 23, 2020, from https://www.quora.com/How-profitable-is-a-candle-making-business

How to Sell Candles from Home - Online Business Startup Guide. (2019, October 17). EcommerceBuff. https://ecommercebuff.com/how-to-sell-candles-from-home/

Instructables. (2012, January 24). Small DIY Aquaponics System. Instructables; Instructables. https://www.instructables.com/id/Small-DIY-Aquaponics-System/

Investopedia. (n.d.). The Top 6 Benefits Of Starting A Home-Based Business. Forbes. Retrieved May 23, 2020, from https://www.forbes.com/sites/investopedia/2011/06/27/the-top-6-benefits-of-starting-a-home-based-business/#10bddbdf7c72

Kahneman Daniel (2011) *Thinking, Fast and Slow*. New York: Farrar, Straus and Giroux.

Kamleitner, B., Thürridl, C., & Martin, B. A. S. (2019). A Cinderella Story: How Past Identity Salience Boosts Demand for Repurposed Products. Journal of Marketing, 83(6), 002224291987215. https://doi.org/10.1177/0022242919872156

Kenton, W. (2019). Behavioral Economics. Investopedia. https://www.investopedia.com/terms/b/behavioraleconomics.asp

Kirzner, I. M. (n.d.). Market Theory and the Price System. Https://Www.Mises.at/Static/Literatur/Buch/Kirzner-Market-Theory-and-the-Price-System.Pdf

Koch, R. (2018, March 16). The Chicago School of Behavioral Psychology. https://www.thechicagoschool.edu/insight/business/everyday-examples-of-behavioral-economics/

Kramer, L. (2019). How Does the Law of Supply and Demand Affect Prices? Investopedia. https://www.investopedia.com/ask/answe

rs/033115/how-does-law-supply-and-demand-affect-prices.asp

Legi, C. (2019, July 1). How To Create Sustainable Fashion From Recycled Clothing. Www.Forbes.Com. https://www.digitalistmag.com/improving-lives/2019/07/01/how-to-create-sustainable-fashion-from-recycled-clothing-06199289

Loannou, L., & Serafeim, G. (2019, February 11). Yes, Sustainability Can Be a Strategy. Harvard Business Review. https://hbr.org/2019/02/yes-sustainability-can-be-a-strategy

Max. (2019b, July 8). 15 DIY Aquaponic Plans You Can Actually Build. Green and Vibrant. https://www.greenandvibrant.com/aquaponic-plans

Meyers, G. J. (2014, April). Designing and Selling Recycled Fashion: Acceptance of Upcycled Secondhand Clothes by Female Consumers, Age 25 to 65. *North Dakota State University*. Https://Library.Ndsu.Edu/Ir/Bitstream/Handle/10365/23189/Meyers_Designing%20and%20Selling%20Recycled%20Fashion.Pdf?Sequence=1.

Per Bylund. (2015, December 21). Theory to Practice: 5 Ways Economic Theory Directly Affects a Small Business. Business.Com; business.com. https://www.business.com/articles/theory-to-practice-5-ways-economic-theory-directly-affects-your-small-business/

Petro, G. (2019, February 8). Upcycling Your Way To Sustainability. Forbes. https://www.forbes.com/sites/gregpetro/2019/02/08/upcycling-your-way-to-sustainability/

Posner, M. H. (2014, September 5). What Is Business Sustainability And Why Is It Important? - GE. GE Reports. https://www.ge.com/reports/post/96692402429/why-it-pays-for-businesses-to-boost-sustainability/

Radcliffe, B. (2019). A Practical Look At Microeconomics. Investopedia. https://www.investopedia.com/articles/economics/08/understanding-microeconomics.asp

Sullivan, K. (2018, February 13). Sustainable Reading and Publishing: How You Can Do Your Part to Help the Environment. TCK Publishing.

https://www.tckpublishing.com/sustainable-reading-and-publishing/

Thangavelu, P. (2020, April 2). How Microeconomics Affects Everyday Life. Investopedia. https://www.investopedia.com/articles/personal-finance/032615/how-microeconomics-affects-everyday-life.asp

Tarasin, I. (2019, March 29). A beginner's guide to upcycling | Lifestyle. Www.Lifestyle.Com.Au. https://www.lifestyle.com.au/diy/a-beginners-guide-to-upcycling.aspx

The Editors of Encyclopedia Britannica. (2013). Distribution of wealth and income | economics. In Encyclopædia Britannica. https://www.britannica.com/topic/distribution-of-wealth-and-income

To, C. (2009, June 16). 10 Principles of Economics. Wikiversity.Org; Wikimedia Foundation, Inc. https://en.wikiversity.org/wiki/10_Principles_of_Economics

Ultimate Aquaponics Beginner's Guide. (2019, October 29). Go Green Aquaponics. https://gogreenaquaponics.com/blogs/news/ultimate-aquaponics-beginners-guide

Upcycled Clothing: No longer on the fringes of fashion, but now fashion forward -. (2016, April 7). Mannequin Madness Blog. https://blog.mannequinmadness.com/2016/04/upcycled-clothing-no-longer-on-the-fringes-of-fashion-but-now-fashion-forward/

Vukovic, D. (2018, January 17). Complete Guide to Aquaponic Gardening. Primal Survivor. https://www.primalsurvivor.net/aquaponic-gardening/

Wikipedia Contributors. (2019a, January 14). Perfect competition. Wikipedia; Wikimedia Foundation. https://en.wikipedia.org/wiki/Perfect_competition

Wikipedia Contributors. (2019b, February 15). Sustainable business. Wikipedia; Wikimedia Foundation. https://en.wikipedia.org/wiki/Sustainable_business

Wikipedia Contributors. (2019c, February 28). Supply and demand. Wikipedia; Wikimedia Foundation. https://en.wikipedia.org/wiki/Supply_and_demand

Wikipedia Contributors. (2019d, March 7). Microeconomics. Wikipedia; Wikimedia

Foundation.
https://en.wikipedia.org/wiki/Microecono
mics

Wikipedia Contributors. (2019e, March 23).
Behavioral economics. Wikipedia;
Wikimedia Foundation.
https://en.wikipedia.org/wiki/Behavioral
_economics

Wikipedia Contributors. (2019f, May 1).
Purchasing power parity. Wikipedia;
Wikimedia Foundation.
https://en.wikipedia.org/wiki/Purchasing
_power_parity

Wikipedia Contributors. (2019g, October 10).
Information asymmetry. Wikipedia;
Wikimedia Foundation.
https://en.wikipedia.org/wiki/Informatio
n_asymmetry

Wolla, S. A. (2017). Why Are Some Countries
Rich and Others Poor? | St. Louis Fed.
Stlouisfed.Org.
https://doi.org/https://files.stlouisfed.org
/research/publications/page1-
econ/2017/09/01/why-are-some-
countries-rich-and-others-poor_SE.pdf

How to Make Money in High School and College

Best Money Making Methods as a Teen and Student, Building Your Own Apps, Selling E-books, and More Easy Side Job Ideas

Clement Harrison

Introduction

"I'm a great believer in luck, and I find the harder I work the more I have of it."

-Thomas Jefferson

This was a quote from one of the founding fathers of the United States, and I would say he was a pretty smart man. This quote is still relatable today and will certainly relate to what we will discuss in this book. The harder you are willing to work, the more opportunities will come your way. The more opportunities that come your way, the greater chance you have for positive results.

This book is written for high school and college students. While reading, you'll discover several ways to earn money on the side that will accommodate your schedule and allow you to use your skills. The market is actually saturated with side jobs, or side hustles, available for just about anybody, even if you have no particular skill set or work experience yet. One of the main reasons students have had difficulty maintaining work while going to school is they could not find employers who could work with their schedule. Those who did not have the benefit of getting help from family members often had to choose between work or school.

There is a better way. Imagine having numerous side hustles right at your fingertips that you can pick up and start doing today. If you have a free evening, work a few extra hours. If mornings are better for you, then that's also an option. If you have a few hours in between classes, then guess what? You can earn a few extra bucks. Does this sound too good to be true? Well, it's not. These opportunities do exist; people just are not aware of them.

This book Exposes these opportunities right here and now. In addition to the schedule convenience, there are a diverse number of jobs available, from online business to manual labor. Whatever may be your forte, there will be a side hustle available to you. There is a plethora of work available out there, and there are only two prerequisites: Have the ability to be flexible and possess a strong work ethic. One thing I am not promoting here is a get-rich-quick scheme. This is anything but that. You will definitely have to put your hours in.

Some Cold, Hard Facts

Being a student is not easy. On top of worrying about your studies, you have to contend with what you will do to pay off your loans after college. This becomes a financial burden for many adults as they spend the rest of their lives paying for their education. Short of getting their loans forgiven somehow, they will have to work them off. This is not easy to do, as the many numbers we go over will show you.

The statistics showing the student loan debt as of 2020 are astronomical. Around 45 million students are borrowing money to go to school. Their combined loan numbers equal around 1.6 trillion dollars (1.56 to be exact). This makes student loans the second-highest consumer debt category behind mortgage debt. As recently as 2018, the student loan debt for the average person was $29,200, which was a two percent increase from the prior year. This does not count the money to be paid in interest. (Friedman, 2020)

Having to pay these loans back is not the only issue. Student loans can affect your ability to buy a house or car, save for retirement, or pay for other emergencies. Many students either can't leave home at any point or have to move back with their parents, since they can't afford the student loans and rent at the same time. Since college students are just entering adulthood, many do not possess acute financial skills to keep their money matters straight. Depending on the type of career you go into, you could be paying off student loans for the vast majority of your life.

Having this debt hovering over you is, at the very least, a nuisance.

This is a serious financial crisis, and until we figure out how to get rid of loans or reduce the cost of education, I don't see this issue resolving itself soon. This is not what we are here to discuss today. I want to help you from falling into the debt trap by being able to make some decent side income. Whether you want to be rich or not is beyond the point. If you don't, that is okay. I am simply here to show you how to be financially independent so you don't have to rely on anyone, whether it is your parents, siblings, friends, cousins, partner, etc.

Whether you care about making money or not, you will need to have it. On top of your student loans, you will have to worry about lodging, utilities, health insurance, food, gas, emergency funds, and many other financial obligations life will throw at you. It's nice to be able to handle all of these independently without seeking out help from others.

I personally experienced major financial matters thrown at me while I was a student. However, I was able to pay rent for an apartment near my work, buy temporary health insurance until my work's insurance kicked in, and get caught up on monthly bills before I even started my job. This is because I already had enough money saved up. It gave me a gigantic head start upon entering the real world.

Beyond reducing your debt, having a side gig or hustle will have a tremendous amount of benefits. It is truly a hidden treasure in the workforce. They will give you a major leg up during life in general. Here are some additional reasons to consider adding some side hustles into your life.

- It is empowering to have multiple sources of income. The traditional route in the past was to rely on one company to provide a living for you. Due to many changes in the economy, and the uncertainty that comes with relying on one paycheck, a person feels like they are in much more control when they have multiple sources of income. Imagine a scenario where you have five sources of income, whatever they may be. Now imagine losing one. You still have four others you can rely on and maybe even give more focus to. You will be able to focus more on the four remaining sources, and, since you are already in the side hustle mindset, you may be able to find another one easily.

- You can learn a new skill or several, and you may even be able to find a whole new career from it. Side hustles allow you to learn something without having to put all of your eggs into one basket. Imagine how many new things you can learn in this manner. This will become much more apparent as we begin discussing specific gigs.

- I have mentioned this already and will continue to point it out throughout the book, but saving money and gaining wealth is a major benefit here. You will learn the value of money and gain some amazing money management skills.

- Having side hustles to grow your finances will improve your stability. This will have a major positive impact on your mental health. Money, or a lack of it, leads to feelings of insecurity. When we have more money available to us, we are in a much better state mentally because we will have less fear and worry. I am not saying that money will cure mental health; numerous factors contribute to it. I am just suggesting it can ease the volatility of our minds.

Side hustles started off as small ways to make extra money. These gigs often lasted a short while until people could get back on their feet. Also, there was a very limited amount of side gigs available. With the explosion of freelance, independent contractors, and temporary work, these opportunities have grown immensely. Many individuals create full-time work and income from side hustles and never have to work a job with a regular schedule again.

How This Book Will Help You

Now that we have discussed the value of side hustles, how can this book help you? First and foremost, I will provide dozens of money-making ideas that will vary in skill level, experience, interest, time commitment, and of course, pay rates. This book will cover a wide diversity of gigs that you can start doing as soon as possible. If one idea does not work for you, there will be several others to choose from.

Not only will you discover numerous side hustles, you'll also learn how to get started and even the steps needed to find customers. I will help you stand out and entice the best clients for your work. At the end of this book, you will know how much you can charge for various jobs or projects so you can always earn what your skills are worth. I don't want you to feel shortchanged, nor do I want your clients to feel ripped off.

This book will not just contain a lot of theory. It also contains real-life stories from other people who have become successful side-hustlers. You will truly get to learn from experience. Finally, once you make that extra money, you will need to know what to do with it. There is no sense in making extra money if you are just going to spend it irresponsibly. Make that dough and use it to build a better and more stable life.

While I cannot prepare you for every single issue that may arise, after reading this book, you will be prepared to take on a new world. You will begin looking at money and work in a different manner. You will become the ultimate side-hustler and be prepared to diversify your work portfolio.

Who Am I?

I have been talking to you about my ideas, but I have yet to properly introduce myself. My name is Clement Harrison and over the years as a bestselling author and business owner of Muze Consulting, more than 200,000 people read my material to discover how to use psychology and systematic methods to unlock the door to business and personal success. That could mean finding a job you love, earning more money, starting your business or mastering the intricacies of your mind.

I started my business while I was studying Neuroeconomics at Princeton. Since I came from a family that did not have much money to spare, I could only afford college by paying it for myself. That's when I decided to discover how money makes the world go round.

While I was at college, I kept hearing all these "advices" from specialists in the field of finance and I found out that experts often tell you how to do something but *they never really follow their own advice.*

I was certain that there were better options to live a more rewarding life if we could use the way our mind works to concentrate on what is actually effective. Not just in business but also on a personal level: in health, social relationships, work, money management and more.

Since then, I've been testing and sharing my findings with the world via my business and books. I love what I do because I've made my living by helping people from all walks of life to become successful and thrive in today's world.

Chapter 1:
Neighborhood Jobs

A neighborhood is a community of people, homes, and businesses that make up a small living space within a region. As you walk around your own neighborhood, you will see children playing, people mowing their lawns, going out for walks, mingling with one another, and even doing community events together. A neighborhood is a place where you live within a certain set of rules, both morally and legally. There is a lot that you can see as you walk around your local community. However, there is something else I will bring to your attention, and that's opportunity.

That's right, opportunity. Your local neighborhood is filled with jobs and projects that need to be completed, and people are aching to have someone fulfill those needs. The variety of these jobs is endless. You may not know about them because you did not know where or how to look for them, but they really are everywhere. You probably have seen many people in your surroundings performing them already. The guy next door offering to shovel peoples' driveways for a small fee is performing a side hustle. The guy who lives in a big city block who moves peoples' cars for them is performing a side hustle. Many of your neighbors are taking advantage of the side hustle phenomenon, and I will showcase how you can too.

The great thing about neighborhood jobs is that you already know a lot of your potential clients. You may be friends with them, see them out and about, waved at them, or at least heard of them. You will not have to travel far to find decent work. One thing to consider is avoiding stepping on peoples' toes. Don't start stealing customers away from other people in your neighborhood. For example, if there is already someone doing landscape work for a particular house, find a different house to go to. Respect an individual's space. The last thing I want is for you to get into a neighborhood conflict.

Neighborhood Jobs

The book is geared mainly towards high school students, so I will be focused on jobs that are suitable for teens. Obviously, certain jobs and projects have age restrictions on them. As I break down individual jobs, I will provide as many details as possible so you can be informed. This section will break down the experience level and skills needed, working conditions, pros and cons, the average pay rate, etc. Once you learn of the many opportunities there are just on your own block, you will be thrilled to get out there and make some extra cash. Again, the most important requirement for any of these is that you are willing to go out there and do the work.

Dog Walker

Have you seen these kids walking around the neighborhood with about five dogs on a leash? If you are an animal lover, you probably think about how lucky they are. The truth is, those probably are not all their dogs. These people are actually working and making an income. Dog walking jobs are a thing, and people can make great money doing them while providing a wonderful service for the owners and the dogs. Dogs need exercise and fresh air, and owners often don't have the time to do it for them—at least, not as much as they would like.

If you are not an animal lover, this may become quite challenging. Enjoying the company of animals is certainly a large criterion that needs to be met if you choose this path. You will literally be surrounded by animals and the more money you want to make, the more exposure you will need. If you are an animal lover, then this side hustle may be right up your alley. Of course, this is not the only qualifying criteria. Not all people who love children should teach elementary school, and not all people who love dogs should be dog walkers. While no previous experience is needed to become a dog walker, there are many things you should take into account.

Before you jump into dog walking as a career, consider some of the pros and cons. Weigh all of these against each other and determine if the pros outweigh the cons. From here, you can decide to proceed forward or not. We will start by discussing the cons.

- First of all, you have to find clients. This is true of many side hustles, so you may not want to weigh this too heavily. However, people have strong relationships with their animals, which will make the process of finding clients who trust you quite difficult. Marketing yourself can become a full-time job on its own. Your best bet may be to start with people who know you well, and then they can let people know about you through word of mouth. Once people realize how good you are, many will seek you out on their own. I would also advise creating a website or at least going through various online platforms like social media to get the word out. Old-school methods like using flyers, emailing directly, or cold calls can also be beneficial. Whatever you

193

decide to do, be proactive with your marketing. It does not matter how great of a job you do if no one knows about you.

- Your income will be variable and unpredictable. Unlike a regular job, where you receive a paycheck every pay period, dog walking income is not set nor guaranteed. Even if you build up a steady number of clients, there is always the possibility of cancellations for whatever reason. Clients may move or decide they do not want your services anymore. There may be a reason why you can't personally perform the duties for a while. For example, you may get an injury. The bottom line is your income is never fully guaranteed, so take this into account. No matter how many clients you adopt, never ditch your marketing efforts, because you never know when you may need them.

- You may have to adopt the "rain, sleet, and snow" motto of the post office here. This means that inclement weather cannot always keep you from your duties. I am certainly not saying to go out when it is severely dangerous to do so. However, realize that the sun won't always shine brightly on your walks. To keep a steady income and maintain the trust of your clients, you must be consistent and not allow the weather to dictate your business. Buy some good snow shows, a warm coat, some gloves, and a hat, and keep on doing the side hustle. Here is something to consider: When the weather is bad, many people will refuse to go out. You may actually gain more clients because of your work ethic.

- Cleaning up messes can get, well, messy. If you have ever taken a dog on a walk, then you know how many messes you have to clean up. That is just one dog. Imagine having to do it for multiple dogs. It is certainly something you will get used to, but it can be off-putting at the beginning. If you have a weak stomach, proceed with caution.

- Dogs do not last forever. This can be a hard fact to take for those of us who adore animals. Over time, you will build a strong bond with a dog. At some point, the owners may move away, or the dog will inevitably pass. When this happens, it can be difficult to take. The pain will be major, but will eventually subside. Other great dogs will be in your life too.

- Animals can get quite wild. Even if a dog is well trained, they are still dogs and can lose control at any point. It is hard to tell how a dog will react to certain things, like other animals, noises, new sights, or people. It is essential always to be alert, no matter how familiar you are with a dog.

If you choose this as a side hustle, also consider becoming a pet sitter. You will have many more opportunities for work, and, with the skills you already possess as a dog walker, it will be a smooth transition for the most part. I hope I have not scared you away with the cons. There are numerous benefits that come with being a dog walker too. We will now go over some of the pros.

- I already mentioned the obvious one, and that is the fact that you will be around dogs all of the time. If you are a dog lover, you will be in heaven with all of your furry friends.

- You will meet many friendly people too. Inevitably, you will develop a relationship with the dog owners. As you get to know them, you will develop a bond over your love of animals. They will promote your business better than anybody if you do a good job.

- You will get plenty of exercise. In addition to walking, handing the tags will create a workout on its own.

- You will get plenty of fresh air and discover new parts of your city.

- Dogs love you unconditionally, and, when they are happy, it is almost impossible not to be happy yourself.

- Instead of dealing with office politics, drama, and complaining, you will be dealing with dogs licking your face. I know which one I would rather have.

- The schedule will be flexible. If you have more time early in the morning, then walk the dogs early in the morning. If you have more time in the afternoon, do it then. Workout the best schedule between you and the clients and get going.

- Once you build up your business, you can make pretty good money and even more than what you would make working full time.

Before you attempt walking multiple dogs at a time, start with just one and move up from there. This is a great side hustle to get into and if it sounds like something you would like to get into, then let's get started finding some clients.

We mentioned before the power of word-of-mouth. This may be the most effective sales technique out there, and it's essentially free. People will just have to like you enough to be willing to talk about you. Other effective methods include community bulletin boards, social media pages, freelance websites like Thumbtack or Fiverr, dog-walking apps, and networking with other dog walkers. If your local community has a newsletter, definitely utilize it if you can. There are plenty of free and low-cost methods to advertise your services. Take advantage of all of them. If you already have a strong presence in your community, this will be a big advantage.

Timing can also be important. For example, people may be looking for dog sitters during major holidays or travel seasons. Use this time to find clients you can build a relationship with. If they are impressed by you, they will come back for your services.

Besides some advertising expenses, there are a few other expenses to take into account. You will definitely need some comfortable shoes and clothes for any type of weather. Consider the terrain that is near you. If you live near a lot of hiking trails and mountains, you should definitely have the shoes that will allow you to go on them. Of course, you will need some good leashes. You don't want to take a chance with a cheap leash, because it can easily break on you. This will create a whole other set of problems, including safety issues for you, the dogs, and the general public. You will also need bags to pick up dog poop. Finally, have a few dog-healthy treats on hand, just in case.

Once you start getting clients, remember that you are representing yourself and your new-found business. Make sure you are reliable, friendly, and hardworking. Be ready to answer questions and be somewhat flexible with clients' requests. You must be trustworthy, because people will be leaving their pets in your hands. This is a big responsibility that you must take seriously. Show up on time and do not cancel unless you absolutely have to. If you must cancel, give as much advance notice as possible. When you offer to walk a neighbor's dog, they depend on you so they can get other things done. Do not let them down.

The final thing we will discuss is payment. Dog walking is hard work and you certainly want to get paid for it. If there are other dog walkers in your area, try to find out what they are charging and stay competitive with your rates. The hourly rate will vary depending on the state and also the economic status of the community you are in. Of course, the last thing you want to do is price gouge people. The goal is to make money without taking advantage of people. According to care.com, the average hourly rate is around 16-18 dollars per hour. One benefit you can give to your clients, which will also be a great advertising technique, is to offer referral bonuses. This means you will save your clients money in some way if they bring you additional customers.

Dog walking is an exceptional side hustle and also very rewarding. If you love dogs and feel a special kinship with them, this gig may be right up your alley. If it's not, don't worry. There are several more opportunities we will go over.

Rating's System Summary:

Experience level: Zero to very low

Time commitment: Medium

Pay rate: $$$. You will earn a decent living if you are willing to put in the hours.

Car Washer

Car washing is a great side hustle, especially in the summer when the sun is out. Anyone in high school or college could have fun doing this job and would do well at it if they are motivated. What is one of the most common things you see when high school kids are trying to raise money for something? In many cases, it is a car wash. It seems like a natural transition for many to make this a summer job. The main qualifying criteria is that you pay attention to detail, you enjoy working with your hands, and you have a strong work ethic.

Washing cars is not an easy gig, especially when you start getting into detailing, waxing, and cleaning the interiors. One car can take several hours when you first get started. Don't worry, because you will get faster and more efficient with time. However, do consider the time commitment it will take when you start this side hustle. It will take a lot out of you, but being in that hot sun with water flowing all over you can be quite refreshing. If you love cars and are meticulous about keeping them clean, consider becoming a car washer.

Just like anything else, consider some of the pros and cons and weigh them against each other. If you are willing to put up with the negatives to bask in the positives, then it is time to get started. The following are some of the cons of starting a car washing business.

- It will be a seasonal business. At the very least, you will make the most amount of money during the warmer seasons and take major pay cuts during the colder seasons. Inclement weather will put a stop to your car washing on any particular day. People will not pay for car washes just so

CLEMENT HARRISON

the rain, sleet, and snow can dirty them up again. Consider where you live and determine how profitable of a business car washing will be year-round.

If you live in San Diego, Phoenix, or Orlando, then chances are you will be able to make great money throughout the year. If you live in a place where poor weather dominates for several months, consider how much profit you will lose during these times. One way to offset this can be to work as much as you can during warm weather so you can afford to take days off during the cold.

While you certainly don't control the weather, clients will be upset if they constantly get their car washed, only to have it rain or snow later. Even though the weather is unpredictable, do your best to assess what it will be like for a couple of days and determine if washing a car is appropriate.

- There can be a lot of equipment involved if you are doing more than cleaning the exterior. This equipment can get expensive to repair or replace when it breaks.

- Finding clients can be difficult. There are many car washing and detailing shops around every corner. It is often easy to drive-thru quickly and get what is needed. You need to offer clients a reason to hire you. Providing service at their home is a good incentive.

- Damage to the car that occurs while you are cleaning it will become your responsibility. Even the smallest scratches and dents can hit your pocketbook in a strong way. Great care must be taken throughout the whole process to prevent damage from happening.

Consider these cons of starting a car washing business. We will now discuss the pros.

- It will be a great exercise. Anyone who has ever washed a car thoroughly knows how much manual labor is involved.

- With the various movements used for cleaning, detailing, and vacuuming, you will eventually work out your whole body.

- This will be a great cash business. As you increase your clientele, you will bring in a lot of income. You could potentially make hundreds of dollars a day. Take advantage of this when the weather is good.

- There is a lot of flexibility involved. If you have a regular job or go to school, you can take advantage of your days off by washing some cars. You can even do it in the morning, evening, or after work or school.

- Fresh air and sun are good for you, mentally and physically. You will get plenty of it as a professional car washer.

- You will get to meet some great people who will become your clients, and you will also get to see some great looking cars.

Assess these pros and cons and determine if you are choosing the right path for yourself. This is a great side hustle once you get started. Before you get your first client and even before you start advertising, there will be a few things you will need. While there won't be any overhead costs if you will be using either your clients' or your personal driveway, there are a few items you need to have.

First of all, you'll need a good hose that will stretch a long distance. You may be able to borrow one from the client, but there is no sense in inconveniencing them in this manner. It is better to just get your own. In addition, you need all of the supplies for cleaning and washing the exterior and interior. This includes something that is safe to use on the body of the car, plus something to clean the tires and wheels. You will also need a good window cleaner and something to take off the bug stains. Those can be pesky and difficult to remove. In addition, many products are needed to clean the interiors like the dashboard and placemats, as well as a good upholstery and leather cleaner. Finally, a solid vacuum that will also help you get into the hard-to-reach places in the car is essential.

Your initial investment may cost you a few hundred dollars, but you can make that up in a couple of days if you are busy enough. These supplies are needed so do not try to skip out on them. If you initially plan to clean the exterior only, then you don't need to buy all of the cleaners for the interior. If you want to increase your business and income potential, then cleaning the interiors is something you should eventually consider. However, starting with just the outside of the car is an excellent way to get your feet wet, both literally and figuratively.

Once you have the supplies you need, then it is time to market yourself. Be very clear about what services you provide. If you don't plan on doing interior cleaning yet, then don't advertise it. Use Facebook and other social media outlets to get the word out. Using Instagram to post pictures of clean cars is a good option too. If your community has a newsletter or bulletin board, then utilize those as well. Word of mouth will go a long way. If people are happy with your work, they will let other people know about you. So, do good work. Finally, keep your own car clean. If you are seeking out clients to clean their car while your own car is a mess, then your offer may not look so good on the surface. Always be professional, friendly, and fair when dealing with clients or potential clients.

Two or three cars in a single day is a good starting point. It is not simply rinsing the car off with a hose. You really have to get in there with a good rag or sponge and get into all of the crevices. The car must be shiny all around for the clients to be truly impressed. Once you get quicker and more efficient, you can increase the number up to four or five and beyond in a single day. Determine how many cars you can clean in a single day while still doing a good job. Eventually, time factor will not be as important as the quality of your work.

A car washing side hustle can bring you in quite an income. You can either charge by the hour or the car. If you are only cleaning the exterior, then 10-15 dollars per car is a fair price. If you will also clean the interior, then 50-60 dollars per car is fair. If you plan on charging hourly, then anywhere between 20-25 dollars per hour is acceptable.

I failed to mention earlier one of the greatest things about doing a car wash side hustle, and that is the fact that you can wear your bathing suit while doing so. Ditch that work uniform for some swim trunks and flip flops. I would tell you to roll up your sleeve, but you won't have them if you're wearing a tank top or t-shirt. Whatever the case, get ready to make some money.

Rating's System Summary:

Experience level: Low. Basic knowledge of how different cleaners work is needed.

Time commitment: Medium. You will need to put in a decent number of hours to make a good extra income. If you can commit 10-15 hours in a week, then you can receive a part-time income.

Pay rate: $$$. Once you get a lot of business, you will be bringing in some good money.

Lawn Maintenance

A good way to make some extra income is by doing some old-fashioned yard work. Children figure this out pretty early as they are out there at a young age mowing their own lawns. Lawn care and maintenance are a great way to make some extra income, especially if you are willing to diversify what you will do. For example, you can mow lawns during the summer, rake leaves during the fall, do general clean up during the winter, and prune trees and bushes during the spring. While lawn care is seasonal to a degree, being willing to perform several different tasks will be a big plus for you.

This kind of work is a fit for any able-bodied teenager in high school and college. You can easily work on a few lawns over the weekend, or whatever your days off would be. If you enjoy manual labor and don't mind getting your hands dirty, then consider lawn care as a side hustle. When doing lawn care, one thing you need to be mindful of is going into someone else's territory. There are plenty of people who do lawn care and maintenance as a full-time career, so the last thing you want to do is take away their business. Focus on people who still need help and also stick to what you can do.

There are certain lawn maintenance and landscaping jobs that don't require a high level of skill, but there are others that do and may even require training and certification. For example, any type of plumbing or electrical work should be avoided if you do not have the experience to handle it. Also, building things like decks and fountains should only be done by professionals. Even work like pouring fertilizer or certain chemicals requires knowledge based on what is healthy for particular lawns and plants. Stick to work that involves manual labor like raking leaves, mowing the lawn, picking up debris, or cutting edges until you become more experienced with the science behind lawn care. There is a reason certain people's grass looks greener. It is not just the time they put in but the techniques they use too.

There are many pros and cons to starting a lawn care side hustle. As we go over these, determine if it's something you are willing to get into. We will start with the cons first.

- Major injuries are a possibility. I am not just talking about cuts, blisters, and bruises here. You could also injure your back, a limb, or any other vital part of your body. You will be handling some equipment that is dangerous too. Be well-prepared and do your research before you use any type of machinery.

- You may have to work with many different chemicals. Be careful about over-exposure and avoid staying in restricted spaces while using them. Also, take great caution to prevent getting these chemicals in your eyes, oral cavity, open wounds, or any other orifice.

- The initial investment may be higher than other side hustles. You need to make sure you have solid equipment and even some backups just in case. For example, you may need two lawn mowers to prevent one from getting worn out.

- Lawn maintenance is not as straightforward as you think. There are a few things you should research or get training for before you attempt them. I also advise you don't do them for the first time in someone else's yard. Stick to what you know.

- Extreme heat exposure when working outside can lead to heat exhaustion and heat stroke, which is a medical emergency. Keep yourself well-hydrated and never go to a job without having enough water with you. If you feel yourself getting too warm, take a break and cool down for a little while.

- Finding clients can be difficult since there are many professionals out there who have been doing it for years.

These are some of the negatives of starting a lawn maintenance side hustle. We will now discuss the pros and hope they entice you into taking on this gig for extra money.

- You will get plenty of fresh air and exercise. It is no secret that lawn care requires a lot of manual labor. This can give you a better workout than going to the gym.

- There are plenty of people who either dislike or don't have time to care for their lawns. If they can find someone else to do it for them, it will make them happy.

- There is a large variety of work you can do. While lawn maintenance is seasonal in many ways, with the wealth of available projects, you can perform it year-round if the weather is at least decent. You can even offer to shovel driveways during the winter.

- The money you bring in is good. People are willing to pay for lawn care as long as the work is performed well. The more jobs you are willing to do, the more money you can make.

- Just like with any other side hustle, you will have a lot of freedom. Eventually, you can create a whole new business out of this side hustle.

- Lawns require a lot of upkeep, so you will get consistent work.

If you are ready to start doing some lawn maintenance work, then let's get going. Remember, you are simply doing this as a side hustle for now. While there are many different jobs you can perform, offer just a few simple ones you know how to do. Determine what those will be and then start gathering supplies needed. A good portion of lawn care is mowing and edging, so it's important to have a good lawn mower and trimmer. If you plan on using fertilizers or other products on the lawn, learn the proper method for using them and when the best time to place them on the lawn is. For example, fertilizer works best when used during certain times of the year. Figure out what services you will provide and get the proper equipment for it. Take into account things like oil and gas for the mower.

You must also take your own safety into account. Buy high-quality gloves to protect your hands. Also, buy sturdy shoes that cannot be penetrated easily and goggles for eye protection. I recommend wearing a mask to prevent inhaling too many chemicals or debris. Avoid using dangerous equipment you are not trained to handle, like chainsaws. Employ whatever safety measures you can; do not shy away from them.

Once you have the supplies and equipment you need, start advertising your availability. Seek out neighbors who seem busy and often let their lawns go from time-to-time. They may need the most help with upkeep. If you know them personally, you can knock on their door. Also, utilize community newsletters and bulletin boards. Look on freelancing websites like thumbtack or Fiverr and use social media. If you go on Craigslist and look for services needed, there are countless people looking for lawn care projects to be completed. You can also make a professional website through Weebly or Wordspace, and flyers to place in designated areas. Do whatever you can to let your services be known in your community.

As long as the weather is in your favor, you can perform lawn care duties throughout the day. Early mornings are an excellent time to start as it will still be slightly cool. Be aware of any noise ordinance rules our neighborhood may have. Do not mow the lawn at 6 a.m. if you are not allowed to before 8 a.m. Only water the lawn during designated hours. Understand these rules and any other scheduling restrictions, and then go from there. Once again, as a side hustle, various tasks can be performed around yours and the client's schedule. Make sure you have enough time to complete a project before starting it. Do not mow half of a lawn in the morning and the rest some other time. Your best bet is to do it on your days off or make sure you have at least a few hours to spare. This way, you can perform the jobs needed and then have time to clean up.

We will now get into the money you can make. Honestly, this depends on the jobs you are willing to perform. You can certainly charge by the actual project, like $30 for mowing the lawn. If you plan on charging an hourly rate, then 30-40 dollars per hour is acceptable. Get ready, because you will be working hard. It will be rewarding though.

Rating's System Summary:

Experience level: Low-Medium. While many jobs do not require experience, certain projects may require training or at least a little bit of research.

Time commitment: Medium-High. Once again, this depends on the project. Expect to be at a house for at least a couple of hours when you're going to do some lawn maintenance.

Pay rate: $$$.

Babysitting

Babysitting is another popular side hustle for high school and college-aged students. With today's crazy work schedules and the fact that both parents need to work in many households, these types of jobs are abundant. If you have time at all during the day, you can use it for babysitting someone's child. You don't have to be a parent to be a good babysitter either. You simply have to love kids and also be very responsible.

Many people think they enjoy being around kids until they are actually around them for an extended period of time. Before you jump into this as a side hustle, I recommend spending some time around children. You may have brothers, sisters, cousins, or friends who have kids. You may also have younger siblings. Assess how you are around them and determine if babysitting is something you are ready to get into. You must have a lot of energy, patience, compassion, and love. Children will bring all of this out of you. Once you are a babysitter, I can almost guarantee you will find someone in your neighborhood who needs one. We will go over a few pros and cons so you can make an informed decision. We will start with the cons first.

- Some children can be quite frustrating and misbehave constantly, no matter what. Their parents are often more difficult to deal with. They may be the reason children display poor behavior. It is certainly not your place or responsibility to tell parents how to raise their kids. If you cannot tolerate the environment, then it's best to just move on. There are plenty of kids who are angels.

- Kids are full of energy and will certainly take a lot out of you. Chasing them around for a couple of hours can be exhausting.

215

- It is a huge responsibility you are taking on when watching someone else's kids. You must be vigilant at all times.

- Children that you babysit for a long time will eventually grow up. It can be very difficult to say goodbye when they do. If you are lucky, they will keep in touch.

- Kids can get hurt physically and emotionally. This can be a hard sight to see.

We will now get into the pros of babysitting.

- Children can be a lot of fun, and the best part is you get to have them for fun and games and then turn them over to their parents at the end of the day. Be aware, though, that some parents expect you to keep their kids on a strict schedule. In the end, you must follow what the parents want.

- The side hustle comes with flexible hours and you can make your own schedule. Parents can be desperate at times and will take whatever schedule they can get.

- There are not a lot of prerequisites to being a babysitter. That being said, it is advisable to have basic training in CPR, first aid, and the Heimlich maneuver.

There are plenty of organizations like the Red Cross, the American Heart Association, and EMS Safety Services that offer various courses. Your local community centers may also offer complimentary classes once in a while.

- You can make a pretty decent side income, especially when you have more than one client.

- You can save on a gym membership because you will get plenty of exercise chasing kids around.

- If you enjoy watching cartoons and children's programming, then you will have an excuse to do so.

- It will help you learn responsibility.

You really won't need any tools or supplies with you, unless you want to bring some games or forms of entertainment for the kids or yourself while they are napping. If you are babysitting at the parent's home, you can generally just use what they have. Make sure it is clear to you what you can use in the house and how much range you will have. There is a good chance parents will ask for a background check and other screenings. It is their children you are looking after.

Since this job is very flexible, the time commitment can be whatever you make it. Try to pick times when most parents need to be at work. Also, you can ask what nights of the week parents will need help because they may want to have a child-free night. Ultimately, the commitment is up to you.

Start approaching parents in your neighborhood, especially the ones you know, about the babysitting service you offer. Also, advertise in community newsletters and bulletin boards. You can create a website or social media page as well. There are numerous websites you can go to that advertise babysitting jobs specifically. These include care.com, seekingsitters.com, or urbansitter.com. If you are trained in things like CPR or first aid, it will make you more marketable.

Once you start getting clients, then you are ready to jump in and get going. You will have a great time getting to help raise a child. Children certainly have a way of bringing out the positive energy in someone. After working with them for a while, you may get a new outlook on life.

Depending on where you live, you can charge anywhere between 12-18 dollars per hour. If you can put in at least 10-15 hours a week, then you can make a pretty good side income. You can certainly charge more, like 20-25 dollars per hour, if you are looking after multiple kids at a time. You may even be able to make a full-time career out of this if you choose.

Rating's System Summary:

Experience level: Low

Time commitment: Low

Pay Rate: $$$

Housesitting

This can be a pretty cool side hustle, especially if your neighbors have some nice houses. This gig is exactly what it sounds like. You will live in and watch over someone's home while they are out of town for whatever reason. You will also keep the home tidy and safe. As a teen, you will likely just stay there for a few hours during the day, unless you set it up where you will sleep there overnight. People often worry about their homes while they are away. Having a reliable house sitter can ease some of their anxiety. Believe it or not, some people actually travel the world and do this as a career. Since you probably still live with your parents, we will stick to your own neighborhood for now.

Honestly, there is very little experience you need here. You just need to be reliable, trustworthy, and responsible. Before you take on a gig, make sure it is clear what your responsibilities are. Will you simply monitor the home, or will you also be cleaning, working in the yard, taking care of pets, etc. Be very clear about what the expectations will be, especially before you negotiate your price. The following are some of the cons of being a house sitter.

- It can be hard to tell what you are walking into, especially with someone else's home.

- You may never truly feel at home, because you will be in someone else's home.

- Maintenance and repairs on a home can become your responsibility to get fixed while the owners are away. You won't be financially responsible, of course. You will just need to set up appointments and take care of the logistics.

- It may seem like two or three side hustles in one if you are also cleaning the yard and taking care of pets.

- If you damage the home in any way, you will be responsible.

There are many pros to being a house sitter.

- You can live in luxurious homes for free and even get paid for it.

- If you are in college, this is a great way to live rent-free without moving in with your parents.

- There is really no upfront cost as you will simply be living in someone else's home for a while.

- You get experience taking care of someone's home, which will build responsibility for your own home someday. Basically, you learn to be a homeowner.

- You can focus your attention on various projects and not have to worry about paying rent and various other bills.

If you are responsible, clean, and want to save money while also doing a great service for someone, then house sitting is right up your alley. Imagine not only living in a house for free, but actually getting paid to do so. Once again, discuss with the homeowners exactly what your arrangement will be. Will they need you to be a live-in house sitter while they are gone or just take care of the house a few hours a day.

Time commitment can be whatever you decide it to be. This will all be arranged between you and the client. You may be needed for a few hours each day, 24/7 for a short while, or even as a permanent house sitter until you or the client decide to move on. If clients own multiple homes, they may need you to stay in one on a permanent basis and simply take care of their property.

According to housesitter.com, most house sitters charge between 25-45 dollars per hour. Some simply don't get paid and live rent-free with food options. Decide what is best for you and negotiate your price. This is a great side gig and the best financial benefit you will get here is saving a lot of money.

If you are ready to become a house sitter, then begin reaching out to people in your neighborhood. Start small and offer to take care of peoples' homes when they are at work, or even on vacation. If you are aware of someone in your neighborhood who is having trouble keeping up their home due to travel, a busy schedule, or any other reason, then offer to take care of small projects or simply live in the house while they are away. Approaching someone upfront about this may seem awkward. People may think it's weird for someone to randomly come up to them and ask to stay in their home.

To avoid the awkwardness, post about your services online, through community newsletters or bulletin boards, and through various sites dedicated to house sitting. Housesitter.com may be a good option to get your name out there. Going through these dedicated sites can also help to keep you safe by hooking you up with reliable people. Your clients will have some peace of mind too. A background check may be needed before you begin. Once you find clients, you are ready to start.

Rating's System Summary:

Experience Level: Low

Time Commitment: Medium to high, depending if you are a live-in house sitter or not.

Pay Rate: $$

I tried to provide a good overview of what a side hustle is and how you can find them in your neighborhood. There is so much more I can go over. However, I have provided you the information you need to get started. Your own community is full of jobs and once you seek them out, they will become abundant.

If you are still confused after going through all of these side hustle options, don't worry. If none of these tickle your fancy, there are many others out there. Go online and search for people who are looking for help with something. You can find people who need help moving, someone to house sit, a personal driver, and many other tasks almost anybody can do. Get creative and start searching your community for work. You are bound to find something.

Chapter 2:
Offer Your Skills

My hope is that you have some ideas for work you can find near your home. These are quick ways to start making some money. If you are not interested in what we went over in chapter one, or if you want additional work ideas, then there's no need to limit yourself. One of the great things about side hustles is that they are in abundance once you know how to look for them.

The choices from chapter one require a lot of manual labor and not too many special skills besides a good work ethic. If manual labor is not your thing, there are certainly more options to consider. Of course, manual labor can bring you a lot of joy if you give it a chance. But I digress. In this chapter, we will talk about the special skills you possess and how you can use them to make extra money. Over the years, you have probably learned a few things from either life experience or lessons you have taken.

Think about the various skills you have acquired. Have you been playing the guitar for a while? Are you a great writer? Have you studied martial arts? Do you have artistic skills? Are you a math wiz? Assess yourself and determine what skills you have that you can offer to someone else. Once you do this, the next step will be learning how to offer them. We will go over that. You do not have to be a master at what you are offering. You just have to be good enough to make people want to hire you. If you plan on teaching something, just make sure you know significantly more than the people you are teaching.

I will go over a few special skills that many high school and college students possess to help give you ideas. This will provide you with the foundation you need to determine your own skills. Take something into consideration. If you are 18 years old and not very good at math, you may still be able to tutor this subject because you will know far more than a 12-year-old, unless that kid is a genius.

Money Making Ideas

I will go over five money-making ideas in this section that you can start offering if you have these particular skills. If you don't, then you can at least get some ideas for coming up with your own and marketing them to the public. When you start doing the research, it is pretty amazing the various tasks that people need help with. While offering these skills as a side hustle, you will have the opportunity to hone them and gain even more clients in the future. As you get more experience, your wages can also go up. Here are just a few examples of skills you can offer to give you some ideas.

Graphic Designer

Many people think graphic design simply has to do with art. If they are great at art, they will be great at graphic design. While this is a large portion of it, there is much more involved. Graphic design is defined as the practice of planning and projecting ideas and experiences with visual and textual content. Basically, it portrays ideas and messages in a certain way. For example, business logos, posters with complicated designs, book covers, mobile apps, and websites, are all part of graphic design.

There are many things around us that we take for granted, not realizing the thought that went into them. For example, there may be specific designs on a building that catches peoples' attention, but they do not know why. There are certain logos and designs that are so familiar that people would recognize them from miles away. They may even see a small section of a logo and immediately know what it is.

The field of graphic design is very complex and utilizes all aspects of the brain. Color, form, texture, shape, and size are all elements of design. An average person may see a structure and think it was put together haphazardly; however, much thought and effort was likely put into designing it a certain way. If you are a graphic designer, then you know the skill it takes. If you are not a graphic designer yet, then it may be a skill you want to develop. If you are artistic, creative, and don't mind working hard, then this may be right up your alley.

Before you can start offering this skill to other people, you must have outstanding graphic design and photo editing skills. You must be able to see things in a certain way that other people can't. This gives you the ability to make designs that stand out. Before you can start on your own, you will also need an up-to-date computer as well as good software for graphic designs and photo editing. Adobe Photoshop is a great software for doing this.

Your ideal customers will likely be business owners and entrepreneurs. They often need various designs and logos for multiple things like websites, storefronts, flyers, and business cards. A person starting up a t-shirt business could certainly use your help. Your designs could make a real difference. Even non-business owners may need help with certain logos, and you could certainly be there to help them.

You will have a blast working as a graphic designer. Before you get started, you will need training, which can be through various courses online, at a college, or through a specific training program. Before becoming a freelancer, you will need some experience and be able to showcase a portfolio of your work. This way, potential customers will take you seriously. There are many pros and cons to consider before you take the leap. We will start with the cons.

- Your work will be subject to scrutiny. No matter what you think of your own work, what the public decides is ultimately what brings you prosperity. If people don't like your work, then you won't make an income.

- Editing can wear you out and not be worth the original price you quoted. Be clear from the beginning how many edits will be offered and let them know that anything beyond this will come with an extra price.

- It is much harder than people think. Your clients may not realize how long it takes to create great designs, so it is essential to educate them.

- People will not want to pay you what you are worth. This goes back to not thinking your job is that difficult. You must stand your ground about the price because you do not want to be taken advantage of.

- The market is quite competitive, especially in larger urban areas. Of course, the demand will also be higher. Do not discount the rural areas though.

- The work can become tedious, especially with edits.

We will now discuss the pros of this career path.

- Your work will be noticed by a lot of people because many people are visual. Your designs will stick out.

- You get to use the creative and analytical sides of your brain. While you are coming up with creative ways to shape your logos, you will also deal with various measurements. Your entire mind will be at work here.

- You will have a lot of freedom in determining when and where you work.

- This is a highly skilled profession, and your skills will be coveted by many different industries. There are businesses of all kinds that are looking for design help.

After reading through the pros and cons, I hope that graphic design is a skill you would like to pick up. If you already possess this skill, then I hope you are ready to make some offers to the public. If you are ready, then create a portfolio of your work. In this day and age, it will likely be online, but you can certainly have some physical copies of your designs too. Start advertising on freelance sites like Fiverr, Upwork, and Thumbtack. These various sites have different levels of fees, so be aware of those as well, because they can cut into your profits. Finally, as you get clients, be very clear about expectations on both sides, so nobody gets fooled or taken advantage of.

As far as pay, it really depends on the work and where you live. Most graphic designers can charge anywhere from 25-50 dollars per hour. The time commitment will vary too, depending on the actual work. One job may only take you a few minutes, while others will take you several weeks. Graphic design is a great skill to have and your services will be needed by a lot of people.

Rating's System Summary:

Experience level: High

Time commitment: Medium to high, depending on the work.

Pay rate: $$$

Tutor

Tutoring is not necessarily teaching, but more so reinforcing and clarifying what has already been taught. Many students will fall by the wayside in class, because they cannot keep up with other kids. They learn about a subject in class, but a lot of it goes right over their head. They go home and review the teachings, but it does little to help them. This is where tutors come in and save the day. The goal of working as a tutor is to explain and break down various subjects or topics to make them understandable for their students. Tutors usually work in one-on-one or small group sessions.

If you are someone who enjoys explaining and breaking down things for people to make them more understandable, then tutoring may be right up your alley. You can become a tutor for almost any subject and also at any level. As long as you have a good grasp of the subject, are very patient, and are able to explain things in a very simplistic form, then you have a high chance of being successful. You must also realize that there is no cookie-cutter approach to tutoring. Each individual learns differently, and you must be able to adapt your approach when dealing with each person. You will become better at this through experience.

Even if you are not a whiz in the subject matter, you can still tutor people at a certain level. For example, if you are taking a high-level math class like calculus and struggling, you can still tutor lower-level math classes. There are many students in high school and college who need tutors. A more significant percentage of them are also self-conscious and would enjoy smaller group settings or even private tutoring.

There are many students from different levels of schooling who are looking for help. You can advertise your services through various channels and schools that allow you to do so. You can also search through multiple sites like Thumbtack or Craigslist to find people who need help in various subjects. Also, advertise on social media. You never know when one of your friends or followers will need a tutor.

While much of being a great tutor comes from experience, there are courses you can take that teach you how to explain and simplify different subjects. High schools and colleges offer tutoring programs, so you can try to become associated with those to practice and hone your skills. After this, you can start offering your skills as a tutor to those who need it. Consider some of the pros and cons of being a tutor. We will start with the cons.

- It can take a while to get going, just like with any other venture.

- You will not get through to everybody. No matter how good you are, there will be students who you do not click with. They will not learn from your various styles. As a tutor, this can be hard to take because your goal will be to help students learn.

- Some students will try your patience constantly. Unmotivated people can be difficult to deal with.

We will now go over the pros of tutoring.

- You will be making a big difference in people's lives. Many students would fail if they did not receive personalized attention from a tutor. You may help them achieve their academic goals, and that will be a great feeling.

- The demand for tutors is very high. Therefore, this side hustle can be quite lucrative.

- You get to be your own boss and set up a flexible schedule.

- There are very little upfront costs. In fact, besides a couple of basic office supplies, there will really be none.

- You will develop some wonderful relationships with people.

- If you are knowledgeable in multiple subjects, then you can tutor multiple subjects. This increases your income potential.

The time commitment is really up to you. A session is generally about one hour, but with private or small group tutoring, you can customize this. To make a decent income, tutoring about 10-15 hours per week is ideal and definitely doable. The great thing is, you can fit these sessions anywhere throughout the day. If you have an hour in the afternoon between class, you can do a short tutoring session and make some extra cash. You can meet someone at their home early in the morning or late in the evening. The schedule is very flexible.

As a tutor, you can charge between 20-40 dollars per hour. Tutoring a small child in elementary school may not be as intensive as far as the subject matter. For these students, you can charge a little less. If you are tutoring high-level college courses, then you can certainly charge more. Some tutors even have rates as high as 50-60 dollars per hour. You can make a great side income by offering your skills as a tutor and will have a great time doing so.

Rating's System Summary:

Experience level: Medium to high, depending on the subject matter.

Time commitment: Medium

Pay rate: $$$

Music Instructor

Have you always had a talent for music? Are you able to play an instrument, or multiple instruments, very well? Then you can make some great money by offering up your skills. You can perform in front of a crowd and make some extra money. However, there is another way. If you are a talented musician and also love to teach, then consider becoming a music instructor.

You may have heard of people giving private piano or guitar lessons. You can do this as well and make some extra money. Besides being an expert in the musical instrument you want to teach, you will also need to display patience and have the ability to explain things very well. Remember, other people may not have the musical talent that you do, especially at the beginning. You must be able to come down to the beginner level and provide clear instructions.

As far as experience, you should be very well versed in the instruments you will be instructing on, and also be aware of various teaching methods. If you have experience as a teacher or instructor in any field, this will be a big plus. You will also need to know about reading musical notes and how to translate them to the instrument.

There are plenty of people out there that want to learn a musical instrument for school, a career, or just a hobby. Many busy professional and creative souls alike love music. They will love it even more when they learn to create it. You can choose to focus your attention on a specific group of people, like high school kids, or expand to include anybody. To keep yourself from getting overwhelmed at first, you may want to focus on a small group of people.

The only tools you will really need are the specific instruments you will be teaching and any guide books that can help you with the process. Your students should have their own instruments. Before you go any further, let's discuss some of the pros and cons of being a music instructor. We will start with the cons.

- Difficult students and parents can be hard to deal with. Sometimes, it gets easier once you become used to each other. If not, it may be time to move on and find other students.

- Many times, students are not learning an instrument because they want to, but because they have to. This can cause them to be unmotivated.

- Teaching music can be more challenging than people think and just because you are talented does not mean you can teach it well to others.

- Students will need to practice on their own beyond just your instruction hours. Many of them choose not to.

We will now discuss some of the pros.

- You will get to teach people something you are passionate about.

- As you instruct others, you will build your own skills too.

- You will develop a strong relationship with your students.

- If you are talented in more than one instrument, then you can teach more students.

- You can set up a very flexible schedule.

- Teaching others is very fulfilling, especially something they can enjoy, like music.

- Despite some of the changes in our time, teachers are still very respected.

Since this will be a side hustle, you can set up your own schedule that will work for your clients as well. A single session is usually about an hour, but you can determine that on your own too. If you can put in about 10-15 hours per week, it can provide you a pretty good side income. The average rate from a private music instructor is between 20-40 dollars per hour. You can negotiate the rate with your client and don't be afraid to ask for what you are worth.

The best way to get clients is to reach out to your local community through bulletin boards and newsletters, advertise to local schools and colleges that will allow you to. Go on social media and various freelance sites to search for people looking for lessons, and also advertise through video recordings. For the last one, record yourself playing an instrument and then post it on various sites with an ad stating you are giving lessons. You can even offer complimentary lessons to entice people. Once you start getting clients, you are ready to roll.

Rating's System Summary:

Experience level: High. You must understand your musical instrument well.

Time commitment: Medium. You make your schedule.

Pay rate: $$$

CPR Instructor

Cardiopulmonary resuscitation (CPR) is a valuable and life-saving skill to have that does not, and should not, be exclusive to healthcare providers. The more people that know CPR, the more potential lives will be saved. This is where you come in. Just like you don't need to work in healthcare to learn CPR, you do not need to be in it to teach CPR either. You just have to be knowledgeable about the subject matter and have a love for teaching.

Before you can begin, you must be certified in CPR and then receive your certification as an instructor. There are many different organizations like the American Heart Association, Red Cross, Or National Safety Council that you can become certified through. If you become certified through all of them, then your income potential will increase. Certifications usually stay good for about two years. There is really no experience required beyond this.

Once you acquire the appropriate certifications, then you need to buy some equipment. This includes manikins, an Automated External

Defibrillator Trainer, masks, shields, barrier devices, etc. There are definitely expensive models that you can invest in, but they will run you thousands of dollars. You can buy less expensive equipment that will run you less than a thousand dollars and it will still be effective. Another option you have here is to work through a specific company or training center as an independent contractor. In this case, you usually do not have to buy your own equipment and can just use theirs. Your income potential may be lower though. Decide which one is better for you.

Once you have the certifications and equipment, you can begin looking for students. If you work through a training center, they will set up classes for you. If you work for yourself, then you can utilize various online forums to find clients. Many healthcare professional schools, like nursing schools, physical therapy schools, and medical schools have students who need to be certified. Advertise there if they allow you to. Of course, you do not have to be exclusive to healthcare providers. There are plenty of people in the community who want to learn CPR. The more people that have this skill, the better. Utilize freelance sites like Fiverr, Thumbtack, or Lessons.com. You can also make yourselves available to schools, corporate offices, and community centers.

Before you move any further, consider some of the pros and cons of this side hustle. We will start with the cons.

- While the upfront costs are relatively low, they may still be higher than many other side hustles.

- There are extra training and certifications involved.

- Lugging around the equipment can be tiresome.

- Extensive cleaning and disinfecting measures for the equipment are needed before and after every class.

- Students can sometimes be difficult.

- It can often become monotonous as you will be teaching the same stuff over and over again.

We will now look at the pros:

- Teaching can be fun and you can get very creative with it.

- You are teaching people a very valuable and life-saving skill.

- You can earn a pretty good income from this side hustle.

- Classes sizes are small due to teacher-to-student ratio guidelines. This means you can give more individualized attention.

- You will be working for established governing organizations that will provide you all of the knowledge you will need.

After considering these pros and cons, if you are still interested, then let's get going. Each class is usually about three hours long. With set up and teardown time, you are looking at about four hours. You can easily teach two classes a day if nothing else is going on. Be mindful of the ratios. One instructor usually cannot teach more than three students at a time. If there are more in a group, then you can ask another instructor to join you. The average salary for a CPR instructor is 30-50 dollars an hour. Some even charge per student. For example, if they have three students, they will charge 50 dollars each and make 150 dollars. Not a bad way to earn some extra income.

As far as setting up a class, you can do it at an individual's home, your home, or a designated space that you rent out. The space you use must easily fit the instructor, students, and manikins. Arrive about 30-60 minutes before class for setting up and expect to stay for 30 minutes after for clean up and questions. Once you get rolling, you will have a great time as an instructor.

Rating's System Summary:

Experience level: Medium

Time commitment: High as there will be significant preparation time.

Pay rate: $$$

Freelance Writer

Freelance writing is another service you can offer that will provide a nice side income. You can offer your services as a resume writer, ghostwriter, content writer, copywriter, or general freelance writer. Many people are looking for talented individuals to help them with their writing projects and if you have a knack for this, this gig may be right up your alley.

You do not have to be Ernest Hemingway to take on this side hustle. You do have to have a way with words, display proper grammar skills, spelling, and clarity. You should also display a little bit of uniqueness in your writing, because being a robot that can just regurgitate something like anyone else won't earn you many points. The formality of the writing really depends on the project. With resumes or educational articles, you will certainly need more structure. If you are writing a personal book for someone, then you may have more leeway with creativity. It really depends on the client and what they expect.

If you love to write and feel like you are good at it, then consider this as a new gig to take on. There isn't any formal training involved, but whatever writing experience you have from school or anything else is a plus. I advise that you have a portfolio of writing samples to share as well. You should be knowledgeable about things like APA style formatting and citations. Also, you need to be familiar with various programs like Word or Google Docs. If you plan on becoming a freelance writer through a particular company, then you will have to familiarize yourself with their platform.

Many people out there either do not trust their writing skills or don't have time to create the masterpiece they want. This is where freelance writers come in. You can help someone write a resume to get their next job, you can create content for someone's website, you can write articles and blogs for various organizations, or you can ghostwrite a person's book for them. These are just a few examples, and the opportunities here are endless.

The only tools you really need are a computer and whatever programs are required to create your content. An editing tool to make sure your writing is clear and free from errors is essential. It is hard for one person to catch everything. A second eye is always needed. Once you are ready to get started, search for people on platforms like Fiverr, Thumbtack, and Upwork. You can find people looking for private help on these sites or various writing companies hiring freelance writers.

Freelance writing is a great side hustle that you can literally do anywhere, as long as you have your computer or tablet. There are a few pros and cons to consider. We will start with the cons first.

- Editing can take a lot of time, especially when the client keeps sending the document back for revisions. If you are working with private clients, be clear about how many edits come with the price tag.

- Once people know you are a writer, they will ask you to write small things for them here and there and try to get it done for free. This is common with friends and family. While it is okay to give a helping hand to a loved one, remember that you are running a business and it's okay to be compensated for your work.

- You will be sitting for long periods of time, which can affect your back, posture, and decrease blood flow. Make sure to get up and walk around throughout the day. Also, keep yourself nourished and hydrated.

- The hours can be quite long for each project, especially when it comes to proofreading and editing.

- It is easy to get distracted, especially if you are at home. Limit distractions as much as possible and find somewhere solitary to write. Go to a cafe or library if you need to.

We will now go over the pros.

- Freelance writing can be done literally from anywhere, as long as you have a good internet connection. If you are out of town and want to make a few extra bucks, then see what is available for you.

- Writing is an art form, and you can get very creative with your words.

- The work is plentiful. You may even have friends or family who need something written for them.

- You will meet some great clients.

- You will be able to hone your writing skills with each project. There is always room to grow.

- You can set up your own hours and work whenever you have time.

Depending on the writing project, you could spend anywhere from a few minutes to several days or weeks on a single project. Obviously, a book with extensive research will take much longer than a blog post. Again, the time flexibility comes in great here because you can sit down to write whenever you have a free moment. If you are writing for private clients, you can charge per project, but the general rate is between 20-30 an hour. Hourly rates may be a better option because some projects are more intensive than others.

Once you are ready to get started, begin marketing yourself through various sites, including the platforms we discussed earlier. Create a website or social media page dedicated to your business. Have some writing samples up for potential clients to look at. Be clear about the services you offer and know what your strengths are. Once you start getting clients, set up a schedule and determine what deadlines they need. Don't miss these deadlines because your clients will rely on you. You will have a great time being a freelance writer and will make a great side income.

Rating's System Summary:

Experience level: Medium

Time commitment: Medium to high, depending on projects.

Pay rate: $$$

Do not stop here. These are just a few examples of services you can offer. If there are other skills that you have, consider how you can offer them to the public to make some extra money. You probably have many talents that the public will benefit from.

Chapter 3:
Be Employed

Side hustles are certainly a great way to make money that provides a lot of flexibility. Many people, including teens, are turned off by the instability that it brings. Even the side hustle work is plentiful, searching and advertising can become quite exhausting and time-consuming in itself. Also, you are not guaranteed a stable income like you would with a job. If finding side hustle is not your forte, then there is still the option of being employed part-time through a company. We will go over some employment options that are suitable for teenagers.

Bear in mind that there will be disadvantages to employment over creating a side hustle. The main one will be less independence and flexibility. You will have less busy work to deal with though, like marketing or setting up payment plans. We will go over these in a later chapter.

Employment Opportunities

There are plenty of employment opportunities for teenagers. Several companies around town are looking for young helpers to keep their businesses running. This employment can be part-time, full-time, temporary, or seasonal. Whatever job you can get, it will be a great way to get your feet wet and get experience in the workforce. We will go over some different jobs that are suitable for teens.

Fast Food Worker

This is a very common area for teenagers in high school and college to work. If you enjoy being around people, doing customer service, working around food, and have a lot of patience, then this may be the job for you. There will be a lot of responsibility involved and keeping things sanitary is a must. People are trusting you with making their food. There are no prerequisite skills involved and you will learn what you need to know on the job. The main thing to consider is your personality and how you approach the job.

Eventually, you will need to get quick with the cash register, be able to multitask, stand on your feet for long periods of time, and cook food quickly and sanitarily. If you do a great job, you could be promoted to manager and then have extra responsibilities. At first, though, this will be an entry-level position.

There are numerous fast-food chains you can work at, so do your research and determine which one you like best. Many people who have worked at restaurants claim they started disliking their food because they were always around. Perhaps you should avoid restaurants where you like the food the most then.

Once you get hired, you will simply need the company uniform and a great attitude. I advise that you get comfortable shoes. Working in fast food is a great way to enter the workforce as you will become experienced in many things. Here are some pros and cons to consider before jumping in. We will start with the cons first.

- You will be on your feet all day.

- You will deal with rude customers.

- You may have conflicts with coworkers.

- The job may get boring after doing the same routine over and over again.

- There won't be tips.

- You may get sick of the food and never want to eat it again because you are always around it.

We will now go over the pros.

- You will have great work experience.

- You can learn skills that you can carry for a lifetime, like time management and handling money.

- Shifts can be flexible, which is great for people going to school.

- You can make friends at work that you may not have known through school.

- There is a very high chance of getting promoted. Be aware of the schedule and whether you will have time to take on extra responsibility.

Consider these pros and cons and determine if this is the right job for you. Overall, fast food work is something positive you can put on your resume and a good way for a young person to start earning money. The time commitment really depends on your employer's needs, but expect to work at least 20 hours a week if you are part-time employed. Since the schedules are usually flexible, you can work weekends, after school, or early in the morning, depending on their needs and what works best for you. There are several options when it comes to fast food places to work at.

The hourly rate for an entry-level fast-food job depends on the location. The salary you receive in a major metropolitan area will be different from a small rural town. Research the minimum wage in your location. In some places, it is $7.25/hour; in others, it is $15/hour. The pay can also depend on the company. The current average is about $11/hour.

If you are ready to get started, then begin filling out your application. Since this will be an entry-level job, you will not be required to have previous experience. However, consider the particular skills you have based on your experience and write it down. There are many online job search sites that you can use. If places still allow paper applications, consider going into a location and get face to face interaction. Look out for help wanted signs. These restaurants may be ready to hire you on the spot.

Do not get frazzled if you don't get the first job you apply for. There are many variables in hiring somebody and do not take it personally if you do not get hired. Keep applying until you get that yes. Once you do, you are ready to get started.

Rating's System Summary:

Experience level: Low

Time commitment: Medium

Pay rate: $$

Lifeguard

Becoming a lifeguard is a great option when you're young. You will have a great job, get plenty of exercise, and have a big responsibility. Your goal here is to keep a watchful eye over everybody in the water and make sure everyone is safe. You will also help prevent unsafe conditions by making sure people don't do anything dangerous. If someone is in trouble, it will be your responsibility to save them, whether they are in the water or anywhere nearby.

The minimum age can be as low as 15 to become a lifeguard, but this depends on the state. You will need to be a superb swimmer while also be able to carry someone with you. You will also need to be in shape overall and have basic CPR and first aid certification. You will need to be able to do some training exercises before getting hired. For example, treading water without using arms for one minute, or retrieving a brick and bringing it to the surface. There is a lot of responsibility and you need to be physically and mentally capable of handling it. Most places will require lifeguard certification as well.

One would think this is a seasonal job. However, there are various indoor and outdoor locations you can work at. Any area that has a large body of water is looking for lifeguards, and many different pools and waterparks are always searching too. There are a myriad of options. You should definitely get a lot of experience before attempting to become a lifeguard at a beach where there will be many currents. This is a great path if you love water and enjoy helping people. Saving someone's life is a huge thrill.

Besides the skills you need, there won't be any other equipment required. Your employer should provide you with things like life jackets or swimming goggles. Of course, you can bring your own too if you feel more comfortable. There are some pros and cons to consider before taking this type of job. We will go over the cons first.

- It is not a job you can just jump into. There will be training involved.

- You will get some major sunburns and deal with harsh weather if outdoors.

- Parents will think you're a babysitter and expect you to watch their kids.

- Sometimes, you have to be the bad person and enforce rules like no running or throwing trash on the ground.

- You are risking your life too when saving someone from the water.

Here are some of the pros.

- It is a rewarding job and you will literally be relied on to save people's lives.

- You get to be near water.

- For the most part, people respect you.

- You will be highly trained in multiple skills.

- You will get plenty of exercise.

Being a lifeguard is an exceptional career path you can follow for the rest of your life. The field is really on the same level as other medical professions. The work will be plentiful and you should be able to work whatever hours you can offer, considering the times that the pools, beaches, and waterparks will be open. If you are in school, make sure the company is able to work around your schedule and try to give them whatever hours you can.

The average lifeguard rate is about 9-10 dollars per hour. If you are ready to get started, then obtain all of the certifications and training you need. You can usually get them through various training centers, the American Red Cross, or a community college. There are numerous online career sites, like Indeed, that have lifeguard jobs available. You can also visit specific locations and see if they're hiring. Look for places that are constantly busy and try figuring out the best times to apply, like in the summer. Being a lifeguard can be an excellent job for you while in school.

Rating's System Summary:

Experience level: Medium

Time commitment: Medium

Pay Rate: $$

Golf Caddy

Being a golf caddy is an often overlooked job, but it is a great option for high school and college students. Junior caddies can actually start as young as 14. The job involves carrying the bags of a golfer, cleaning the clubs as you make rounds, and assisting the golfer you're assigned to as needed. All of these activities will be of great help to a golfer.

This job is ideal for a young adult with an athletic build and someone who does not mind some heavy lifting. If you enjoy being outdoors and are a morning person, that makes it even better. There is no real experience or training needed. Whatever tools you need should be available at the golf course. However, you should have basic knowledge of golf and what your responsibilities as a caddy will be. Develop a good relationship with the golfers you'll be working with.

Before jumping into this career, consider some of the pros and cons. We will start with the cons first.

- You will be waking up early. Most golfers like to play in the morning before it gets too hot.

- The golfer you work with may not be the kindest.

- You will be doing a lot of heavy lifting.

- You are essential to a golfer's game but get very little credit.

- It can get very hot at times and the sun will be scorching. Keep yourself hydrated.

- A game may be canceled due to inclement weather, which means you lose out on wages for that day.

We will now go over some of the pros:

- You will get a lot of fresh air and exercise.

- The time commitment is not that much. You can help with one game in a day and work for four hours.

- Golf is a game that attracts affluent people, so you will make some great tips.

- You will develop some unique relationships and can even start networking a little bit.

Going back to the time commitment, if one game takes about four hours, then you can easily fit in two games in a day. You will probably get the most work opportunities during the weekends. The pay rate is anywhere between $20-30 per hour. The real money though comes in the tips. If you help a golfer improve their game, you will get some nice cash awards.

If you are ready to get started, begin looking online for potential employment. Also, visit various golf courses and country clubs in your area to see if they are hiring. Many locations have summer programs.

Rating's System Summary:

Experience level: Low

Time commitment: low

Pay rate: $$$

Retail

Retail is another great option for high school and college students. These types of jobs include clothing stores, grocery stores, pet shops, vitamin stores, and fashion stores. Furthermore, there are various roles you can play within these establishments, like cashier, sales associate, stocker, janitor, etc. Entry-level jobs do not require experience, tools, or training. Of course, you will need to learn the operations of the business, like working the register, once you start your new role. You will also need good customer service skills.

There are numerous employment opportunities, such as the ones we mentioned above. Try to pick out locations you would enjoy working in. For example, if you like athletics, then check out some sporting goods stores. There are definitely some pros and cons to consider. We will start with the cons:

- Rude customers will come in on occasion.

- You will work weekends and holidays.

- You will usually be working indoors.

- You will often be asked to do multiple jobs, like stock, clean, and work the register.

- The pay is relatively low and there are no tips.

We will now go over the pros of this type of work.

- You will gain many different job skills.

- There are many different retail options for you.

- You will get plenty of exercise.

- You will meet some very interesting people.

- Stores often have discounts for their employees.

- There is a lot of room for growth and promotions.

The great thing about retail is that there are varying shifts, so your hours can be flexible. You can work before and after school, on weekends, or even in between classes if you are in college. Many retail stores are close to schools and colleges, so the commute is very manageable.

The pay rate depends on the area you are living in and the minimum wage of the location. Despite the actual job positions, any entry-level role will pay between $7.25 to $9.00 per hour. There are plenty of opportunities for advancement, though.

If you are ready to get into retail, start looking online, or visit specific locations. Look for help-wanted ads too. Some locations are ready to hire on the spot. You can also pick up extra retail work on a seasonal basis during certain holidays.

Rating's System Summary:

Experience level: Low

Time commitment: Medium

Pay rate: $$

Youth Sports Referee

Being a youth sports referee of any kind can be a blast if you love sports. This job will not be for the lazy or unathletic, though. You will be working your butt off and earn your money. You will also need to acquire some skills. First of all, you will have to know the rules of the game you will be refereeing for. You will need to have a pretty strong personality and know-how to be fair. You will also need to know how to take criticism, because you will make many calls that people do not agree with.

To be a referee for youth sports, you will not need too much experience to start off with. You won't need any tools except for the one provided for you on the job, like uniforms, whistles, and flags. It is better to begin with younger kids and then move up the ladder to high school, where the stakes are higher, later on. You will need to be certified through whatever governing body is in your area. This can be a great job option for teens and young adults because of the flexibility. We will go over some of the pros and cons of this job. We will start with the cons first.

- The athletes can be brutal, and so can their parents. You will take a lot of heat.

- You have to be aware of the rules and be ready to enforce them. People don't take kindly to this, especially when the call is against them or their team.

- You are essential to the game but get very little recognition.

- You have to deal with different coaches and their personalities.

- You will deal with inclement weather for outdoor sporting events.

We will now go over some of the pros.

- You get to watch the action in a game up close.

- You will be moving a lot and getting exercise.

- It is a great way to contribute to the community.

- There will never be a dull moment.

- There are many different sports to choose from.

The time commitment for being a youth sports referee is not that high. A typical game for kids usually lasts one or two hours, so you can easily fit it into your schedule. On your day off or during the weekend, you may be able to referee several different games. The average pay rate is between 12-13 per hour and can also vary by sport.

After obtaining your licenses and certifications, you are now ready to start refereeing. Start reaching out to different leagues and organizations in your area and see where they will need you. Places like the YMCA or different recreational centers are a good place to start.

Rating's System Summary:

Experience level: Medium

Time commitment: Low

Pay rate: $$

These are just some of the examples of employment suitable for high school and college students. You may do your research into other options as well. The income potential here is not as great as it is with side hustles. However, these are still good options to make extra money while in school.

Chapter 4:
Create Something to Sell

For this chapter, we will return to the entrepreneurial spirit. There are several money-making ideas where someone can create something and then sell it. These items can include online tools or physical goods that you would like to have.

Making Useful Items

There are many ideas that teens and young adults can take on and create to make a profit off of. We have been seeing this type of ingenuity for generations now. Young people can be creative when they are given the opportunity, whether it is by opening up a lemonade stand, making art to sell, or creating mobile apps during modern times. When high school and college students go this route, they also develop their marketing and selling skills. This can lead to much success with business down the line. This chapter will go over some ideas to help get your creative juices flowing.

Creating an eBook

You have probably seen countless ads out there about eBooks for one subject or another. It seems like everywhere you look, people are putting out eBooks. They are literally all over the internet and range from just a few pages to hundreds. What you may not realize is that these books are being put out by people just like you. They are not world-renowned authors. They are simply people who are knowledgeable about a subject and want to get the information out to the public.

eBooks are a very cost-effective way to earn money on the side. The best part is, you can publish your work immediately without having to reach out to dozens of publishers and hoping for just one response. Anybody can write eBooks. If you are knowledgeable about a subject and feel like you want people to be educated about it, then this path may be right up your alley. Think about the subjects you are well-versed on. It can literally be anything like cooking, bargain shopping, or fixing bikes. Maybe you have gone fishing for several years and feel like you're an expert in it. Write a book about it. If you notice that a subject needs attention, you can even do some research and put it together in a book.

You do not need to be a New York Times Bestselling author here. Basic grammar and spelling proficiency is good enough. Any customer who is interested in the subject you want to write about is a potential customer. It will be good if you can find one or two niches to focus on and develop a repertoire there. People love to get information from a single place and an eBook is a perfect example.

All you need to get started is a computer. You can use the Amazon platform and follow their guide to create and publish your eBook. You can have your book ready to go within days, or sooner if you are a quick writer. There are several other platforms and templates you can use online as well. We will go over some pros and cons of eBook writing for you to consider. We will start with the cons first.

- You will cover the costs of writing an eBook, which are not that high if you are willing to do your own proofreading, editing, and cover design.

- You are responsible for the marketing efforts. There are many sites, like Book Cave, that can help.

- You have to make sure you are as honest and factual as possible to prevent putting out false and inferior content.

- Some people still neglect the benefits of eBooks.

- Indie authors generally do not get the same respect as experienced authors.

We will now go over some of the pros.

- You will have complete control over your book, like where it is sold and how it will be promoted.

- You pretty much have the final word on everything related to your book.

- You will have plenty of support from other indie authors in the same boat as you.

- You get to keep 100% of your net gain.

- Your book will be available on the market much quicker than it would with a traditional publisher.

The time it takes to write an eBook depends on the content, the research involved, and how long you plan on making the book. Once you get better at writing, the quicker you can finish. Publishing on kindle can take just a few hours, or a couple of days, depending on how long the book takes to be reviewed. English titles are published much quicker.

The average earnings from an eBook are about $1,000 in a year. If you write several and on a regular basis, you can certainly make a decent income, depending on the content and marketing. You may not make great money, but it can become a good side income.

If you are ready to start writing eBooks, find your platform and get going. Find the topic you want to write about and figure everything out from there, like the title and content you want to put in it. Also, consider editing and cover design options. If you don't want to do it yourself, you can find people on platforms like Fiverr for relatively cheap. Remember that an eBook does not have to be the size of a novel. Just make sure you fulfill the intended purpose of the book. Once you finish, congratulate yourself for becoming an author!

Rating's System Summary:

Experience Level: Low to medium

Time Commitment: Medium, depending on how often you want to write.

Pay: $

Online Courses

Many entrepreneurial types sell online courses as an extra revenue source. There are several individuals, companies, and educational institutions alike who are going the online course route because it can save so much time and energy in other ways. If you are someone who has a great idea, passion, skill, or knowledge that you want other people to see and learn from, then creating an online course is definitely for you. It is such an excellent way of disbursing information. With the availability of the internet globally nowadays, imagine how many people you can influence.

If you can offer a solution to a problem, then you can likely create a popular online course. You can generate extra income while also providing a great service. Even if you are young, you will have some wisdom to bestow. So, do not sell yourself short. There are plenty of people around the world who will benefit from your teachings, so start creating your online course content. If you have heard of a problem that people are having difficulty solving, then focus on that and create an audience of eLearners. For example, as a younger person, you will have far more knowledge about technology. One idea is to create a course teaching people how to use their smartphones.

Obviously, you will need a computer. Beyond that, having strong knowledge in whatever you will be teaching is a must. You will also need a strong online presence, social network, and email list. Finally, you will need to get on a platform to create your content and do some marketing. The more people that know about you the better. If you have this already, it's a huge plus; otherwise, you can build it along the way. You will definitely spend more time marketing and networking than you will actually creating a course. We will go over some pros and cons to creating an online course. We will start with the cons first.

- You may create something that nobody cares about. It can be hard to gauge what people want and this may cause you to create a course that gets zero traction. Do your research ahead of time and follow trends. Also, try to figure out the most significant problems people are dealing with and come up with content.

- You need to really build up your audience and that can take a long time.

- The eLearning market is getting pretty saturated, but there is still quite a demand.

We will now go over the pros.

- The technology used to be pretty extensive, but now you can use various sites that will set up a sales page for you and even allow you to host your videos all for one low price.

- You own 100% of the content you create and also keep 100% of the profits after some initial investments.

- The courses do not have to be that long to be profitable.

- You will be able to teach and influence many people. Imagine someone from the other part of the world benefiting from your teachings.

The time commitment here varies tremendously based on how extensive and long the course will be. It can take anywhere from 20 hours to hundreds of hours. In addition, you will be doing a lot of marketing to make the public aware of the course. The money you will make is also dependent on how much you can sell the course for and how many people will buy it. At first, you will probably just make enough to have a nice side income. As you improve and sell more courses, you could potentially sell thousands of dollars' worth of courses every month.

Once you are ready to start, decide on your specific course topic based on what you think the public wants. Do the appropriate research that is needed and then outline the course. This includes setting up your goals and objectives and then creating the content. You can then determine your price and begin setting up the course online. After this, it all comes down to your marketing. Additionally, you can begin marketing and building up your audience ahead of time. After your course is entirely available, the income you make will all be passive.

Rating's System Summary:

Experience level: Medium

Time commitment: High

Pay rate: $

Building an App

There seems to be an app for just about anything nowadays. If you can think of it, you can probably search for it in the app store. Many of these apps are created by everyday people who have a great idea. You can build an app for companies to use or mobile apps that can be sold on the app store. People from all walks of life use an app of some sort.

If you are interested in technology and love the major advancements we have gone through, then this is something you can create. Having coding skills is definitely essential. However, there are plenty of platforms today that allow you to work without having to learn how to code. Still, developing this skill set is beneficial. Once you have a great idea, you are ready to go. All you need is a good computer and a platform to help you build apps.

Almost everyone uses an app of some sort. The people who your app will most likely help will be your target audience. Imagine building an app that serves people all over the world. Before we continue, we will go over some pros and cons. We will start with the cons first.

- You have to be technologically sound.

- Building an app can be very time-intensive.

- You may make a lot of money, or none at all.

- Your idea may flop.

Here are some of the pros to consider.

- If the app catches on, you can make a lot of income.

- App building platforms make it much easier than before.

- It may help a lot of people and provide a great service.

The main thing about apps is that building them can take a while. Plus, once you build an app, there will be a lot of marketing to get it well known to the general public. Hopefully, after a handful of people know about it, it will catch on like wildfire. The money you make really depends on the specific app and the users.

If this works out well, it can become a real winner for you. When you are ready to get started, there are a few steps to go through to make it happen.

- Determine what the idea for your app will be and then do the market research to determine if it has potential.

- Create mockups and then design the app.

- Build a landing page and then build the app using a good app platform.

- Once you launch the app, begin marketing it. You can even do some marketing ahead of time to get people excited.

- Once the app is out there, listen to your audience. If they have suggestions for improvement, consider them strongly.

Rating's System Summary:

Experience level: Low

Time commitment: High

Pay rate: $

Selling Photography Online

Selling your photography on sites like Shutterstock or Pexels is actually quite easy. It is also free and can be very profitable over time. After uploading your pictures to one of these platforms, you still retain the copyrights to your work and receive a royalty whenever someone downloads them. If you love photography and also want a way to showcase and sell your work, this will be the perfect opportunity for you.

You will need good photography skills so your pictures will catch people's eyes. You will also need a computer and an account with Shutterstock or whatever platform you will be using. Once you have these, then you are good to go.

People are always looking for stock images to use on multiple projects like books, posters, PDFs, PowerPoints, or just their personal collection. You never know when someone may look at one of your pictures and realize that they need it. This is why it is good to always have something available on a stock photography site. We will go over some of the pros and cons to selling your work through these channels. We will start with the cons first.

- You will make very little money for each picture sold. Usually, it's about 25 cents to start and can go up to 33 cents when more pictures are sold through a subscription.

- They have strict requirements for uploading, so your pictures have to be almost perfect.

- To make good money, you will need to upload a large volume of pictures.

- Slow income growth at first.

Here are some of the pros.

- Once you upload your photos, you will receive all passive income.

- The more exposure you get on stock sites, the more money you will make per picture.

- You will learn and perfect your skills through experience.

- You do not spend any time with clients. They just see your work online and can buy it if they choose.

Once you are able to take perfect pictures, then you can start uploading them through your account. This can take a significant amount of time at first, as you are building up your portfolio volume. The money you make will depend on many factors, the main one being how many downloads your picture gets. The good thing here is the more pictures that sell, the more money you will start making with each picture. For example, once you pass the $500 income mark on Shutterstock, your royalty amount will increase.

Remember, once you upload your photos, they will sit there on the platform and make money for you. Create as many different types of pictures that you can so you get the attention of several different people. You can certainly advertise that you have images online through various social media sites or your own website.

Rating's System summary:

Experience level: Medium

Time Commitment: High

Pay rate: $

Selling Baked Goods

A popular way to make some money, whether for personal income or for charity, is to sell baked goods to the public. Everyone enjoys baked goods, whether they are cookies, pies, cakes, bread, or various other types of food.

Before you jump into this, you will need to have some great baking skills and be able to create many different types of baked goods. Depending on your particular state, you may need a food license and specific permits for setting up. Good baking and customer service skills are the main things you need. In addition, once you have these items, you just need your tools for baking, a large table to set up, and some signs. You may want to buy some new baking ware that is up-to-date and provides you with what you need.

Your customers will be the people who love to eat. If you stick to local areas and clientele, take suggestions from them on what to make based on their requests. The more you listen to your customers, the more business you will create. There are some pros and cons of selling baked goods. We will go over the cons first.

- You have to comply with state regulations, which can become daunting.

- You must ensure sanitary conditions at all times.

- Developing a rapport with your community to start earning some business.

- Baking for long hours can become exhausting.

Here are some of the pros.

- If you truly love baking, then you may not mind the long hours.

- You get to make the food you love.

- You get to set up your own hours.

- You will meet some interesting people, and they get to try your delicious food.

- Once you establish a rapport, you can tailor to your customers' needs.

The time commitment can get quite extensive, especially once you start getting requests. It is not just the time selling, but also the time baking and cleaning that you need to take into account. It may serve you well to stick to items that are easier to bake, like cookies or muffins. Selling by yourself, you will not make a ton of money selling baked goods. Expect about $400 a month, which is a good side income for a teenager.

Once you are ready to get started and have all of the items you need, then start marketing what you sell and your specific locations. Put a message out on social media, notifying people where you will be and when. Have signs that are very visible. You can even start taking requests and orders ahead of time online. If your baked goods are tasty, you will have customers lining up in no time.

Rating's System Summary:

Experience level: Low

Time commitment: Medium

Pay rate: $

You probably noticed that the pay rate is not that high here. Do not worry too much about this because most of these job types are for passive income. Plus, as you build your name and brand, you will see your income going up. At the beginning, expect your pay rate to be low, but never quit trying to get your name out there.

Chapter 5:
Trade Anything

Are you a good salesman? You should consider selling as a side hustle. There are many platforms you can use to sell anything, both online and in-person. We will discuss several ideas that you can start engaging in ASAP.

Start Trading With These Methods

The great thing about using these ideas is that you can start selling and trading if you know what sells and have it available to you. You don't have to create anything ahead of time, except for a website or page on a particular platform. Besides that, you are ready to start making a profit much faster than many of the ideas on the previous chapter.

Domain Flipping

Domain flipping entails purchasing domain names from various registrars on the internet and then selling them to someone else for a profit to an interested buyer. This type of work is ideal for entrepreneurs who have a good sense of what domain names and words would be valuable to a buyer and popular with the general public.

You can also research AdWords on Google's Keyword Tool. Search for words with the highest tracking volumes and try to incorporate them naturally into a domain name. This way, you are following the trends of society. Research and marketing is an essential skill to have for this side hustle. Besides that, there is no experience required and all you need is a good computer with a domain portfolio management software. This will help you keep everything easy, organized, and efficient.

With the access people have to domains at the top-level, one would think this practice is no longer profitable. However, you can still make a pretty good chunk of change doing this, especially when helping those who are not as tech-savvy or familiar with what domains are. Also, individuals who are running their businesses, both big and small, may not have time for figuring out websites and domain names that work. They are happy to outsource this type of work, and this is where you will come in. We will go over some pros and cons for this type of work. We will start with the cons first.

- You will have to invest money first into domain names before making a profit.

- There is no guarantee of a return on investment, this is why it is important to research words the best you can.

- You will not be making money to make you independently wealthy, but you can still make a pretty good chunk of change on the side.

Here are some of the pros.

- It is easy to get started once you have the tools.

- You don't need to be a high-level technological wiz.

- Once you buy a domain name, it is yours until you sell it. So, you can use it and test it out at first. This may increase your ability to sell it for more.

- You can set up a domain name without having to build an entire website and also get them for pretty cheap.

- You can sell to big businesses, small businesses, or individuals.

There is not a huge time commitment involved here. You just need to do some research before purchasing a domain name, and then some marketing afterward to sell it. The profit margins vary based on the domain. However, the average profit margin is around $2,000 for domains that are sold. Not a bad return on investment for the time and money that were put in. Once again, this is not a guarantee, just something to look forward to.

If you are ready to get started, then you can jump right in. Start researching potential domain names that may be valuable in the future. There are numerous registrars like GoDaddy where you can buy domain names. You can purchase them for as low as $10. Imagine buying 10 at this price for $100 and then selling just half of them for about $2,000. Finally, start marketing your domain name on Sedo, which is a domain auction site. Also, NamePros and DNForum are available as great resources for helpful tips and tricks. Domain flipping can become a great gig for you.

Rating's System Summary:

Experience Level: Low

Time commitment: Low

Pay rate: $$$

Garage Sale Flipping

You have probably been seeing garage sales your whole life as you drive around town. Your parents may have had one. Well, you can make a pretty good profit using a technique called garage sale flipping. How does this work? You basically buy items for a heavily discounted price at a garage sale, and then sell it for a large profit on eBay.

You would not believe how many valuable things people get rid of at garage sales because they do not need them.

Well, if you are someone with an eye for value and are great at bargain shopping, then this is great for you. However, even if you are not, there are tools you can use that will help you tremendously. You don't have to have any experience, but just be willing to do a little bit of legwork. Your customers will be those who you find on eBay. People have been selling items on eBay for profit for decades now, and it's time for you to jump in as well.

Basically, drive around and look at the items they are selling at a garage sale. You can then do a quick search on eBay to determine how much the item is selling for. Once you find an item at a garage sale that catches your eye, go to eBay and search for that exact item. Scroll down to "sold items" in the filters and you can see what the particular product has been selling for. For example, the particular product may be selling for $10 at the garage sale, and people are buying it for $100 on eBay. People will often sell treasure chests without even realizing it.

All you need is a computer, a smartphone or tablet for when you are out searching, and an eBay account. Also, you must have patience because there will be many garage sales where you find nothing of value. We will go over some pros and cons of garage sale flipping. We will start with the cons first.

- You will need a lot of patience.
- Sometimes, you may need to haggle for a lower price.
- You may find nothing to sell.
- The item you purchase may not sell on eBay.
- You will have to ship items yourself.

Here are some of the pros.

- You can make great profits on single items.
- People at garage sales will often sell vintage items in mint condition.
- eBay has a lot of traffic on their site and it's easy to research.
- You just need one or two big hits a week to make some good money. Imagine buying $100 dollars worth of items, and then just one of them selling for $1,000.
- Expenses to buy items can be written off.

The time commitment for this side hustle can be quite high, especially when you are traveling around looking for garage sales. You may have to wait a while for your item to sell once you place it on eBay.

The profits you make can range from $100 to $1,000 or more. The more you sell, the more you make. So, it's pretty simple in that regard. Here's an extra tip. You do not have to limit your purchases to garage sales. You can bargain shop at many places and you will be floored by some of the things you can purchase at a discounted price.

If you are ready to get started, then gas up your car, and start finding some great deals. Set up an eBay account. You may also advertise your eBay link on social media. The more good reviews you receive on eBay, the more potential customers you will have.

Rating's System Summary:

Experience level: Low

Time commitment: Medium

Pay rate: $$

Dropshipping

This is a new wave of buying and selling products online. Through a dropshipping site, you can sell products to customers at your own price, and you don't even have to carry inventory or pay for it until it is sold. Once you have made a sale on an item, the supplier will ship your products directly from their warehouse. It seems like a win-win for everybody. All you need is the entrepreneurial spirit and knowledge of how items get sold through the various sites.

You do not have to have any experience getting started. Once you get set up, you can start selling your products to interested customers. You can focus on specific items and set up your regular customer base, or you can sell a wide range of supplies to target numerous groups. To get started, all you need is a good computer and then set up an eCommerce platform. Here are some pros and cons to consider when setting up a dropshipping business. We will start with the cons first.

- You will have to do research on finding products that sell.

- You will have to rely on other peoples' stock, so finding a good distributor is essential.

- You don't get the bulk pricing for items you want to sell, so you will likely pay more for each item.

- Even though you do not personally handle the products, you will get the blame from many customers if they arrive damaged.

Here are some of the pros.

- You do not have to handle, package, or ship any products.

- You generally don't have to pay for inventory until it is sold.

- Low Startup costs.

- You can update your inventory quickly and have a diverse number of products without having to worry about storing them somewhere.

Dropshipping is great for people who simply want to play the middleman between the seller and buyer. You will be spending some time setting up your store, selecting products, and deciding a pricing strategy before you start selling. Setting up your store is where the majority of the work is. The money you make depends on the hours you put in and the amount of inventory you sell. Some people make well over a hundred thousand dollars a year, but they are selling thousands of products a month. As a student, selling a couple of dozen a month may be all you can do for the time being.

When you are ready to start a dropshipping business, consider the following steps. This may be easier than you think.

- Come up with a dropshipping idea and products to sell. Some people focus on what their passion is. However, you should also research products that are popular and will make you a profit.

- Perform a competitor analysis to determine what your competitors are selling and for how much. You want to stay competitive in the market.

- Find a good supplier. You can find good suppliers from sites like Oberlo, where you can see the reviews and ratings.

- Build a dropshipping business store by setting up a domain name, building your site, and signing up for Shopify, which is the most comprehensive eCommerce store around.

- Market your dropshipping business everywhere, including social media.

Dropshipping is a great business model that has benefited a lot of people.

Rating's System Summary:

Experience level: Low

Time commitment: Medium

Pay rate: $$

Flea Market Flipping

Flea Market flipping is a similar concept to Garage Sale flipping. You can buy various products from flea markets, yard sales, or discount stores, and sell them for profit through platforms like eBay, Amazon, Craigslist, or Facebook. If you love bargain shopping and have an entrepreneurial spirit, then consider this great business idea.

You will need to have a lot of patience and the ability to look for sellable items. Also, you'll need a smartphone or tablet to look up prices for items that you find is essential. For example, if you find an old video game in mint condition, research on eBay or Craigslist to see how much the item is selling for. If the profit is worth it to you, then consider buying for a low price and selling it.

You will have several customers through various online platforms whom you can sell to. You can focus on a few products or sell a diverse number of items. You can also do some market research on what people like to buy. All you need to get started is a computer, smartphone, and an account with the websites we mentioned above. Consider some of the pros and cons of flea market flipping. We will start with the cons first.

- You will have to spend a lot of time and effort looking for sellable products.

- Several products you buy may not sell.

- If you don't do your research, you might pay more than you need to.

Here are some of the pros of this business plan.

- You will have a lot of freedom.

- You will meet some interesting people as you go around shopping.

- You can sell through multiple platforms.

The major time commitment comes from going around and shopping for items. Once you have your inventory, then you must post them online. Make sure you take a good photo to put up. You want the product to look good. If you or someone you know is great at taking pics, then that's a plus. Finally, once the product sells, you will have to package and ship it.

Through flea market flipping, you can potentially buy an item for $10 and then sell it for several hundred dollars. Many people create full-time incomes through this model. For now, your goal is to make a little extra money on the side.

Once you are ready to get started, you just have to set up your various accounts and then start shopping and buying. Post the items you want to sell and wait and respond to customers as they become interested. Make sure to market your business on social media and other platforms as well.

Rating's System Summary:

Experience level: Low

Time commitment: Medium

Pay rate: $$

Selling Your Old Items

You may have a treasure chest in your closet. If you love to sell things and feel like you have valuable products in your home, then you can start decluttering and getting rid of some stuff. Clothes that you have outgrown, toys you no longer play with, and books you have already read are some examples of things you can sell. You can also sell your parents and siblings items, but make sure to ask them first.

The old saying, "One person's trash is another person's treasure" is attributed to this business model. Items that you no longer want may be a necessity for someone else. Hence, you will have many potential customers. Never discount anything you have that may be able to get sold. While some products may not have a great resale value, other vintage items may have gone up in price. Check out sites like eBay and Craigslist to find out what various products are selling for.

All you need is a computer and an account with different sites to start selling. There is no experience required besides the research you will need to do. This is a fairly easy thing to set up. We will go over some of the pros and cons of selling your own products. Here are some of the cons to start off with.

- It can be hard to let go of things due to their sentimental value.

- Some products may sell for less than what you bought them for.

- Decluttering can take a while.

- Profits are limited because you can only sell items that are in your home.

Here are some of the pros to consider.

- You will not need to buy inventory since it is already in your house.

- You can collect a lot of money on your old items.

- You will be able to minimize your belongings and make room for more products if desired.

- You will be helping people by providing the items they need.

The time commitment here is much lower than the previous ideas because you will eliminate shopping around. You will still have to post about your items, market, and then ship them.

Just like with garage-sale flipping, you can potentially sell vintage products for several hundred dollars in profit. Once again, research the market through various sites to determine what specific items are selling for.

Once you are ready, collect the items you want to sell and begin uploading them to eBay, Craigslist, Facebook, and other sites that allow you to sell. When posting about an item, make sure to put any flaws they may have so the customers are fully informed.

Rating's System Summary:

Experience level: Low

Time commitment: Low

Pay rate: $$

Learning to sell through various methods is a great way to start making extra income.

Chapter 6:
Earn from Ads

There has been an online revolution going on in the world for several decades at this point. It has never been easier to connect with people around the world through various online channels. Once you are able to understand how this works, you could create content that will attract a large audience, which can eventually lead to earnings from advertisements.

Creating Content to Attract Advertisers

You may have heard of YouTube stars who have posted videos that generate millions of dollars. It sounds like a great gig, right? Well, it may be harder than you think. The concept here is that you are creating content that will attract an audience. If you can attract a significant number of followers, then advertisers will become interested in paying you to be promoted on your sites. Another great thing about these activities is that they can be fun and fuel your creativity. It can certainly take a while to build an audience, so be patient.

Create a YouTube Channel

A lot of people are on YouTube these days. You can find content for just about anything. When you have a YouTube channel, your goal is to create content that will be attractive to people, whether entertaining, educational, dark, or light-hearted. Once a large number of people view your videos, you can attract sponsors who want to display their ads on your channel.

If you are creative and have some great ideas for videos that will catch the public's eye, you may have found the right path for yourself. It is not always as easy as standing there and talking in front of the camera. You must be engaging, have proper light, great content, and be able to tell a story. Finally, you need to have video editing skills so you can upload a professional-looking video.

There is no experience required beyond knowing whatever you will talk about. You must have good editing software, a computer, and a good camera. The camera on your phone is acceptable. You may want a higher quality one later on. Some YouTubers also invest in selfie sticks that rotate on their own to provide better views and angles. If you make great videos, you will attract viewers who are interested in your content. Even if they are not interested in your content, they may just like you as a personality. Consider some of the pros and cons of being a YouTube personality. We will start with the cons first.

- It takes time to build an audience that you can monetize.

- It's a highly competitive market.

- May need to spend additional money to create quality content.

- Some of your content may get demonetized if it does not follow the guidelines of YouTube.

- You may get very few to zero subscribers.

- You need to be over 18 or have parental consent to be on YouTube.

Here are some of the pros.

- Potential for huge passive income. Once you have a large following and sponsors, each video you create could bring in large sums of money.

- Work and create content whenever you want.

- Create content you are passionate about.

- Have the ability to help and influence people around the world.

You may want to choose a niche market to focus on. The time commitment can be high, especially when trying to build an audience. Also, creating, editing, and uploading a video can take a while if you want them to look professional. YouTube requires a minimum of 1,000 subscribers, and 4,000 viewing hours before you can monetize and join the partner program.

The top earners on YouTube make millions of dollars. It will take you some time to get to that level, but keep working for it. Initially, you will just be making a small chunk of change.

You can get started by using the following steps:

- Find a niche or specific content you want to focus on.

- Create a YouTube account. Think of a unique name, icon, and art that goes along with your content.

- Begin making and uploading content and playlists.

- Start sharing your content. Do not rely on YouTube to market you. Post your videos anywhere you can.

- Analyze the data, like which videos are getting the most responses.

- Stay engaged with your audience. Follow the comments and answer questions if you can.

Rating's System Summary:

Experience level: Low

Time Commitment: High

Pay Rate: $; low at first with the potential to become a millionaire.

Creating a Blog

Blogs are websites that focus on written content, like articles or short blurbs. Bloggers often write from a personal perspective. There are numerous types of blogs on just about any type of content. Just like with YouTube, your goal is to create content through writing that will attract followers. Once you have enough followers, then you can bring in sponsors as well. If you are creative, and enjoy writing content of any kind, then blogging is right for you.

You do not need any experience before starting a blog beyond being knowledgeable in whatever content you decide to create. All you need to get started is a computer and a creative writing mind. You can literally write on anything. Some people choose educational posts, while others choose entertaining ones. You can have a combination of all. Search around and see for yourself how many different blog types there are. Consider some of the pros and cons of creating a blog. We will start with the cons first.

- You will have to do a lot of writing before getting noticed.

- You may or may not ever get noticed.

- People will be critical of your work, especially if you have controversial topics.

- It is quite a saturated market, but you can still stand out.

Here are some of the pros to consider.

- You will be able to publish your content immediately.

- You will get to practice your writing skills.

- It's a great medium to express yourself.

- You will find many like-minded people.

The time commitment can be high at first while you are creating your website. After everything is set up, you must write blogs regularly. Being absent can cause your audience to become concerned or disinterested. An article can take around 30 minutes to write, depending on the content and how fast you are.

The highest level bloggers can make hundreds of thousands to even millions of dollars. Article clicks essentially pay you once you have sponsors set up. You can make around $0.01-$0.10 per article click. It will take a while to build up your audience and start getting sponsors.

If you are interested in blogging, here are some steps to get you started:

- Choose a platform to begin blogging. WordPress is the most popular one to use. There are reasons that so many people love this platform, and that's because it provides many benefits. Other options are Blogger or Tumblr.

- You can set up a free blog or pay a fee to create one. If you pay, you will have some advantages, like owning your domain name. There are different levels of fees, depending on the services you want.

- Design your WordPress page to your liking.

- Start blogging and creating content.

Rating's System Summary:

Experience level: Low

Time commitment: Medium

Pay rate: $

Podcasting

Podcasting has revolutionized the way the spoken word is used. It has even replaced old-school radio and many media outlets as well. People often trust podcasters more than regular journalists these days. There are podcasts for almost any topic you want, and it is easier to start one than ever before. As of June 2020, the market is still not nearly as saturated as blogging. If you are someone who loves talking on-air and has something valuable to share, then podcasting may be the right forum for you.

There is no real skill required. You just have to be able to talk, convey your message, and attract people with your words. This is actually more difficult than it sounds, especially when you are talking to people through various online channels. Your customers will be your listeners, so determine what subjects you want to talk about and what is popular at the moment. Chances are if you like something, many others will too. They just don't know anyone has the same interests.

You don't need a lot of high-tech equipment. In many instances, you just need a phone, computer, and a decent microphone for voice quality. After that, several platforms can be used to create a podcast. Consider some of the pros and cons of podcasting. We will start with the cons first.

- It will take a while to build an audience.
- You will not get to see the reactions people have to your words.
- Talking for long periods can be exhausting and if you don't have enough content, there will be a lot of dead air time.
- You may not have any listeners at all.

Here are some of the pros.

- You can talk about what you love.
- You will be able to interview guests who you enjoy talking to if you do an interview-style show.
- You can get creative and truly discuss almost any topic.
- You will have fewer regulations than other media outlets.
- You can decide the lengths of your shows.
- It's easy to record almost anywhere.

There can be quite a large time commitment for podcasting, especially when it comes to coming up with content, researching, editing, and uploading. Oh yeah, you also have to record content too. Your commitment also depends on how often you do the podcast. Your audience will not enjoy long periods of absence.

Eventually, when you have enough viewers, sponsors will become interested in you and start paying for ads. If you make it big, you can make millions of dollars. Think about the Joe Rogans of this world. Of course, you do not have to become Joe Rogan or Adam Carolla to be successful. You can build a nice audience of a few thousand people and make some decent side money. It will take a while to even get to this point. Remember, your podcast can be available worldwide.

If you are ready to get started, then take the following steps:

- Choose a topic, or topics, that your podcast will cover.

- Consider getting a co-host to bounce things off of.

- Choose a catchy name for your new show.

- Determine the format, including length, style, show introduction, and the closing statements.

- Set up your equipment and choose a podcasting platform, like Podbean or SoundCloud.

- Begin recording your show. Edit the show before uploading through the platform.

You can have a great time doing a podcast and start bringing in some passive income.

Rating's System Summary:

Experience level: Low to medium, depending on how high-tech you want to become.

Time commitment: High. This also depends on the show's length and how often you will record.

Pay: $

Instagram Influencer

Instagram has become an amazing social media website where people can share their pictures for other people to see. You can become an influencer on Instagram once you've established a large audience and credibility. For example, numerous fashion influencers can encourage many people to buy a piece of clothing simply because they are promoting it. It's like when a celebrity wears a dress on the red carpet and the sales spike almost instantly.

If you love Instagram and don't mind documenting aspects of your life on it, then you can also become an Instagram influencer. Once you have a major following and credibility, various brands will swoon over you to help sell their products. You can make a pretty good chunk of change by simply posting great photos of yourself. The top influencers make millions of dollars. It will take a while to get there. For now, any side income you can make will be a blessing. Your customers will be your followers.

There is no real experience required, you just have to be able to influence a large number of people to do something. For example, some influencers can create excitement over a hotel and cause people to want to go there. This can take a while to do, and I will provide a few tips later on. Your best bet is to follow other influencers and figure out their tricks. You must have a computer, an Instagram account, and a good camera. The camera on your phone should work if you know the tricks. There are some pros and cons to consider when becoming an influencer. We will start with the cons first.

- It will take a while to build an audience.

- Your personal life is somewhat on display.

- You must upload the perfect picture.

Here are some of the pros.

- You can make passive income once you become an influencer.

- Many people will trust you.

- You have the potential to reach a lot of people.

- There are many influencers you can follow.

- You can influence people while living a luxurious lifestyle.

You will have to put in a significant amount of time while building your audience. You will always need to be aware of good opportunities to take a good picture. You are essentially always working and influencing people.

To start making money, you will need many followers. As you increase your followers, you will also make more money per post. For example, an influencer with 10,000-100,000 followers can earn about $200 per post. Any more than this, and it can go up to over $600 per post.

If you are ready to become an influencer, then take the following steps:

- Think about what makes you unique and capitalize on it. For example, you may be a great comedian or cook.

- Get rid of your insecurities and don't be shy. You have to let your audience into your life. Of course, there are things you can still keep private.

- Document your life; don't create one.

Document many of the things you do regularly through photos.

- Stick to a particular aesthetic so your audience can follow you.

- Invest in a good camera and maybe even photography lessons.

- Make yourself available for sponsorships.

Rating's System Summary:

Experience level: Low

Time commitment: High

Pay rate: $

Affiliate Marketing

Affiliate marketing is the ability to earn commissions by promoting other people's products. If you find a product you like, you can promote it to others and earn a percentage of profits for each sale. There are products you use every day that you can promote. The merchant of the product will give their affiliates a link they can put on their sites. If an individual clicks on the link and purchases a product, they can track the link it went through and give commissions. You can also receive a commission if a buyer delays purchase.

The more followers you have, the more commissions you can make. There is no experience needed. You just need to be familiar with the product since you are putting your name to it. You just need a computer and any type of site where you can post the affiliate links. You can even use your private Facebook page. Your customers will be whoever follows you. Consider some of the pros and cons. We will go over the cons first.

- You have no control over the affiliate markets that exist, so you just have to use the ones there are.

- You don't establish a customer base. A repeating customer usually won't purchase from you again.

- There are no revenue guarantees.

- People may feel like you are spamming them.

Here are some of the pros.

- Low investment costs.

- It's a billion-dollar business.

- There's a lot of convenience and flexibility.

- You don't have to deal with customer service.

- The vendors provide marketing materials, so you don't have to create your own.

You can start making money as an affiliate marketer almost right away. However, the commissions will be low for a while. High-level earners can make over $3,000 in a day. When you start out, you may be making just a few dollars a day and may get up to a few hundred a day if you stick with it.

To become an affiliate marketer, consider the following steps:

- Review products in your niche. Consider the products you use and love.

- Build an email list with your prospects on it. Email is still a great marketing channel.

- Educate your audience with webinars and other educational tools to keep people informed about the products you are affiliated with.

Rating's System Summary:

Experience level: Low

Time commitment: Medium

Pay rate: $

I put a low pay rate on all of these ideas because you will not make a lot of money to start. Once you build your audience, you will have the potential to make a lot of passive income.

Chapter 7:
Getting into the Nitty Gritty of Making Money

Throughout this book, we have gotten into various ways for young students to make money through many different side hustles and forms of employment. Look at the different types of work we have described and determine if any pique your interests. If they don't do that, maybe they will at least open up your mind and give you new ideas. One of the major objectives of this book was to give you a whole new perspective on how to make money that is not traditional. There is a wealth of work out there that will allow you to make more money, so take advantage of this.

Administrative Responsibilities

For this chapter, we will discuss an often overlooked section of side hustling, and those are the administrative responsibilities. It is not just limited to working and making money. There are numerous things you need to take care of behind the scenes to make sure the jobs you take on go smoothly.

The first thing you must do is figure out what jobs and side-hustles will pique your interest. If there are multiple ones that do, then don't be shy about taking on several different ones. Of course, make sure you do not overwhelm yourself. I have no idea what your school schedule is like. Look at it for yourself and determine what hours work best for you and what days of the week are most convenient. Make sure your clients are fully aware of the time commitment you can give them. School needs to remain your priority. The income you make from these types of jobs is simply icing on the cake.

Inexperienced freelancers have a hard time determining what they should charge. My advice is to research the market conditions in your area and what freelancers who are doing similar work also charge. Be aware of the value you bring to the client based on your skill level and experience. Do not shortchange yourself and also do not purposefully try to cheat the client. This will do nobody any favors. Decide for yourself if you want to charge by the hour or per project. Honestly, it depends on the specific type of work to determine which option is better for you. For example, mowing the lawn could be per project, but clearing weeds could be charged by the hour. Just make sure you and the client are both clear about this.

I recommend that you sign an official contract for the work you agree to do. You can find freelance contract templates online that include sections for your name, the client's names, the work to be done, the agreed-upon payment, and other essential terms and conditions. Many freelance platform sites already offer contract services and mediums to communicate with clients. If you are not using a freelance platform, then please make sure a contract is signed. Also, keep track of any written communication through email or texts. This is to protect you and the client. The last thing you want is to deal with legal issues that could have been avoided.

As far as receiving payments, you can certainly go the old-fashioned way by taking cash. Make sure to keep a record of the cash you take in and deposit it immediately for security. We will discuss this more later. Please look into more advanced payment intake methods as there are plenty. For example, you can install a tool that attaches to your phone so that you are able to take credit card payments. There are plenty of credit card apps on the phone too.

PayPal is a popular and secure method of taking payments. Other methods can be CashApp or Square. I advise that you don't set up automatic payments yet and simply charge when you are about to do the work. For projects that will take a long time, like days or weeks, cut it down into payment plans. This way, the client will not be burdened with one huge payment, and you will feel secure knowing that you are getting paid for your work.

Invoices should be maintained for the work you do. You can easily create these online through various sites, including directly on PayPal. Invoice your clients promptly so that you remain up-to-date for the work that you do. This will ensure that you keep good records too. Establish some guidelines on late payments. You can certainly be flexible now and then, but make sure you put in specific deadlines for payments that the clients are aware of. Also, make sure they know about the fees associated with late payments. You have a right to get paid on time. I hope it never gets to this point, but if the client refuses to pay you, you can turn the matter over to a collection agency. This is why it's important to keep good records.

I have mentioned these throughout the book; however, take advantage of freelancing and side hustle platforms like Fiverr, Upwork, Thumbtack, Freelancer, and even Craigslist. Countless job opportunities are available on these sites, and you can even market your own services on them to find potential customers. Creating your own website is also a plus. Social media can be utilized as well and you can create quite a following on these various sites. You can even make a separate business page if you don't want to deal with the social media drama.

I advise you to attend local networking events where people can learn about each other, develop relationships, and recommend each others' businesses. Finally, the old-school methods of word-of-mouth and email are very beneficial. It is hard to believe that email is now an old school method, but it has been around for a while. It is still an effective marketing tool. You want people to talk about the great work you do. Real-life stories help sell products and services.

The hardest thing for new freelancers to do is to negotiate. It can be intimidating, and the thought of losing a client can be difficult to deal with. One thing to remember is that you are offering a valuable service. Charge based on your experience, values, and end results. Your work should speak for itself. It is okay to negotiate down on a price, but always set a minimum rate you are not willing to go below. Neither you nor the client should feel cheated during the transaction. Try to negotiate other things besides just price, such as offering a small extra service for loyal customers. You can even offer discounts for early payments—whatever you can afford to do and still make a profit.

Taxes

Taxes are never a fun thing to think about, and it never becomes something people enjoy doing. It is part of the game though, and you cannot avoid it. Even minors have to pay taxes. You may as well start learning about it early. Whether you work for an hourly wage at a job or perform various side hustles, you will not get to keep everything you make. Until they somehow change the system, this will be a reality.

If you work for an employer, they will have you fill out a W4 and other appropriate tax documents. You will have a certain amount of money withheld from your check every time, which are the taxes being deducted. If you are a minor, your parents could help you fill out the paperwork. During tax season, you will receive a W2 form, and the information needs to be filed with the IRS. From here, the government will determine if you need to pay more, or if you paid too much and will get a refund.

If you are doing unofficial jobs, like the side-hustles we mentioned throughout this book, you will have to keep very good records of all of your earnings and expenses. Certain items that you spend for your business can be tax-deductible, so definitely make sure to keep track of them. In addition, money from investment accounts, gifts, or inheritances all needs to be reported. Basically, if you make any type of money at all, the government wants to know about it. If you are making money through some type of side hustle, remember that taxes are not being held automatically. You must set a good majority of it aside to pay out your taxes later.

If you are under 18, you should discuss filing for taxes with your parents. There are several online programs, but you can also hire a professional. This is something for you to decide, and I will not recommend one way or the other.

Taxes can certainly seem like a burden. Most of us would much rather keep all of the money we make. Educate yourself about the importance of taxes and what they are for. Ask your parents for information too. The roads we drive on, the schools that are built, the post office, and various other programs and services are funded by tax dollars. They are essential to keep the country moving. Once we understand the purpose of taxes, it becomes easier to accept them being taken out of our accounts.

The End... Almost!

Reviews are not easy to come by.

As an independent author with a tiny marketing budget, I rely on readers, like you, to leave a short review on Amazon.

Even if it's just a sentence or two!

So if you enjoyed the book, please...

leave a brief review on Amazon.

I am very appreciative for your review as it truly makes a difference.

Thank you from the bottom of my heart for purchasing this book and reading it to the end.

Chapter 8:
What to Do With Your Money

We have gone over many ways to make money. What's amazing is the variety of ways we can make money from credit devices, mobile apps, PayPal, and various other online platforms. My goal for this book was to get young students more educated about money. This does not just mean bringing more in but also learning to save and helping it grow.

I will not be giving you specific financial advice here. I will be teaching you about the value of money and the importance of not wasting it. It is painful to see so many individuals make countless amounts of money that most people cannot even imagine, only to spend it completely and have nothing to show for the future. Poor financial habits are detrimental, no matter what career path, or paths, you end up choosing. Before you worry about making extra money, focus on managing what you have. Otherwise, no matter how much you make, you will always be broke.

Before we get into specific money management techniques, let's swing back around to the various money-making options we have discussed. You may have noticed that several of them can be done in less time than others while also being very flexible. As you enter into the working world, I want to encourage you to set yourself up so that you have more than one source of income. With the volatile job market we live in, it is difficult to rely on one source of income. Furthermore, there are too many ideas out there for us to ignore. If we neglect taking advantage of so many opportunities, we are doing ourselves a great disservice.

Here is another thing to consider. You can use the various sources of income to fund different areas of your life. For example, you can take the income from one source to put into your savings account and the income from another source to pay bills. Having more than one way to make money will help put you at financial ease.

Saving Money

Here's the bottom line: if you do not learn to save money, you will spend all of it and always end up broke in the end. Your salary and income can continue to increase, but if you don't fix your spending and financial habits, it will not matter in the end. You may get a few thrills and buy some toys along the way. However, this will not matter much when you have to sell things to make some of your money back. I am not telling you not to have fun. You work hard for your money and, of course, you should enjoy it. I am just saying you don't have to spend all of it to be happy. You have to save up for the future.

The first thing we must do is set up a budget. This is where you determine your expenses and income and assess if you are bringing in more money than you spend. If you are not, then you need to make some major shifts in your finances. This means you need to reduce some of your spendings, figure out a way to increase your income, or a little bit of both. Setting up a budget can be tedious. However, it is necessary if you are to manage your finances properly. We will go over the steps to creating a budget. Make sure to write everything down so you can see it visually.

- The first thing you must do is calculate your expenses. Add up all of your expenses every month, whether it be from eating out, monthly bills, insurance, payments, or any other expenses. There are some payments that you may not have to make monthly, like car insurance. This is why I suggest adding up your total expenses for six months to a year and then dividing by the number of months. For example, if your total for six months is $8,000, then divide by six, and you will get your average monthly expense rate of about $1300.

- A good rule of thumb is to calculate what 10-15 percent of your monthly income is and then add it on top to get your total. For example, 10 percent of 1,300 is 130, so your total monthly expenses are $1,430. This strategy will account for any miscellaneous expenses that may have been missed.

- Next, determine what your monthly income is. Calculate all of your income that you may be receiving from jobs, side hustles, allowances, etc. Add all of these income sources together for one month. If your income changes month to month, then you can calculate an average as we did with the expenses. We will say your monthly income average is $1,600.

- Take your total income and subtract your expenses. In this case, 1,600-1,300=300. For our example, we are positive and earning more than what we spend. This is a great start.

- Don't be satisfied here. Look for ways to increase income and reduce expenses so you have more money to put away. If your expenses are greater than your income, this is not good. Make some changes right away. What expenses do you have that can be taken out? What can you do to increase your income?

- Revisit your budget report on a regular basis to make sure you are not falling into the red.

Okay, so you have $300 extra per month, which is good. What will you do from here? Stick it in your piggy bank or under the mattress? That's not a bad idea, but what if the money gets lost? It is better to have it in a secure location. This brings us to the bank and setting up your various accounts to keep our money safe. The great thing about savings and checking accounts is that our money is FDIC insured. This means the bank is liable for giving us back everything we put in.

If you are a minor, then you will need someone to open up an account for you. I encourage you to set up multiple accounts and distribute the money throughout all of them. If you keep all of your money in one account, you are more likely to spend it. If you keep it separated, then it is easier to determine what you spend and what you save. We will discuss three types of accounts you can open.

- A savings account can be used to store money away. This is money that you simply save and don't plan on using unless there is an emergency or big expense. A high-interest account like a money market account is good because it will provide you with high yields over time. Remember that savings accounts are set up for just that: savings. They often penalize you with fees when you take money out. So, do your best not to withdraw if possible.

- A checking account is one where you can easily deposit and withdraw with a check, debit card, or ATM. Put all of the money that you plan on spending for any reason into this account.

- Certificates of Deposit or CDs are basically accounts that yield relatively high-interest rates. There are many different types of CDs, so it is best to go to the bank and determine which one is best for you. If you can set up an account like this early in life and deposit for several decades without removing anything, then you will save a lot of money throughout your life. A CD is a nice and safe investment account to open.

As you continue to have income coming in, distribute it throughout all of these accounts. You can decide what percentage you put in each based on your personal finances. The more you put into savings between the savings account and CD, the better. Saving money is a powerful tool that your future self will love you for. When you get into the habit of it early, you are more likely to maintain it for the rest of your life.

One more concept I want to go over is the idea of paying yourself first. This simply means that when you bring in any form of income, put aside a certain percentage of it right away before you use the money for anything else. For example, if you get paid $500, immediately save 10 percent of it, which is $50. Too many people forget to pay themselves first and then have nothing left at the end. Get comfortable with paying yourself first. It is a strategy you must start implementing as soon as possible.

Investing Your Money

Your first goal with money is to save as much as you can. Once you have enough capital, then it is time to start investing too. Investing gives you the potential to grow your money at a faster rate than just saving it. It is a great way to build your wealth throughout life.

The first thing you want to do is reinvest into your business to help it grow and prosper. This means that you should take some of your income and put it back into your various side hustles or work. For example, if you are doing lawn care, purchase higher quality equipment so that you can work on more lawns throughout the day. You can even set up a separate business bank account solely to buy things for your business. You may also place the income you receive from your businesses into this account. This will allow you to keep better track of your finances for tax purposes as well.

There are several safe investment accounts that young students can open up. If you are a minor, you will have to open a joint account with your parents. These accounts include Roth IRAs and index funds. Both serve as passive investment accounts that allow your money to grow at a faster rate than a regular bank account without you having to do much at all. These types of accounts are asset-based, which means the money you put in is distributed throughout various security assets, like stocks, bonds, real estate, and cash. Since your money is spread throughout these various asset classes, it is a much less risky investment strategy than playing individual stocks or purchasing real estate yourself. Once you have enough capital from saving your money, consider starting one of these accounts.

You can open an investment account through a bank or brokerage firm with the help of a financial planner. The financial planner will also oversee your account and reshape it as necessary to make sure you receive the best returns on your investment. Your main goal with these accounts is to work with your financial advisor to determine what percentage of your funds will go in each asset class. The riskier accounts generally have a higher return on investment. The riskier the account, the higher the chances for gains and losses. Contribute money regularly to these accounts so they can continue to grow. Here is a breakdown of how your funds may be distributed.

- Stocks: 40%
- Bonds: 20%
- Cash: 10%
- Real estate: 30%

The main difference between different investment accounts is how they are managed and how they are taxed. Your financial advisor can fill you in on all of this. Your best bet is to go with an established company.

The point I am making here is that your money is valuable. It is hard-earned and the last thing you want to do is waste it by spending irresponsibly. This is completely avoidable if you just change a few money habits. Keep more of your own money by learning to save and invest.

Conclusion

Congratulations on making it to the end of this book, *How to Make Money in High School and College: Best Money Making Methods as a Teen, Building Your Own Apps, Selling E-books, and More Easy Side Job Ideas*. My goal for this book was to introduce to you, the readers, many new ways of making money through avenues you may have never thought of. While the subject matter is geared towards teenagers and young adults, people in their 30s, 40s, and beyond can also benefit from the information provided. Don't let the title fool you too much.

The traditional way of making an income by relying on only one source is slowly going by the wayside. There are numerous opportunities out there for people to make extra income while enjoying a flexible schedule. Also, being able to have multiple sources of income through so many different channels is a blessing for sure. My goal with this book was to introduce you to many different ways you can earn an income while going to school full time in high school and college.

Unfortunately, being a student will not allow you to get a traditional 9-5 job due to the class schedule and school work that you have to deal with. With these non-traditional forms of income, students can make some extra money on the side while still being able to focus on school full time. In some cases, you may be able to earn a full-time income and beyond, even if you are not putting in full-time hours.

Through the various lists of money-making ideas, I hope that you were able to get your creative juices going and think of many ways in your own life that can provide you with some extra cash. You certainly do not have to limit yourself to the options I provided. They are merely suggestions, but definitely something to look into. I tried to make the ideas as diverse as possible to make sure not to exclude anybody. We all have different talents and once we start recognizing them, we can open up a whole world for ourselves. Sometimes, it just takes a little extra motivation, and I am happy to provide that for you.

Throughout the different chapters, I provided an overview of the many ideas that exist out there. For the ones you found to be enticing, definitely do further research. I want you to be as informed as possible, and the main goal of this book was to give you many wide-ranging ideas.

I want to remind you that your skills are valuable. Do not be afraid to charge what you are worth, but try not to take advantage of people. It is a balance and the fairness needs to go both ways. Make sure always to set up your payment platforms so you can start accepting money right away. You do not want to start working and have no way of getting paid. That would defeat the purpose of this whole new route. Always remember to pay your taxes. Definitely keep good records of your business expenses and income. Any income you bring in is taxable. The last thing you want is to deal with the IRS. That is all I will be saying about that.

Finally, once you start bringing in extra money, make sure you are managing it responsibly. It does not matter how much you make if you do not keep any of it. I want you to hold onto as much of your money as you can. My recommendation is to set up your savings and checking account ahead of time and use the "pay yourself first" strategy to load up these accounts with your money. Once you have saved up enough, consider opening some long-term investment accounts too. The sooner in your life that you begin to save and invest, the better financial outcomes you will have for the future.

I hope this book served you well and provided you with a lot of new knowledge you never had before. It is hard to be a high school or college student and not having your own money to use for the things you want. By learning these unique methods to increase your income, you can significantly increase your independence too. Thank you for taking the time to read this book. If you enjoyed it and feel it can help other people, then please write a review, so more people become aware of it. If the information provided here helps as many people as possible, then this book is a true success. One of the keywords throughout the book is "Hustle." If you are ready to hustle, then you will likely be successful!

Join our inner circle

to sign for exclusive bonuses and free offers, including:

- Notification of new releases
- Free audiobooks
- Giveaways
- pre-release specials
- Private Facebook group access
- Video training

References

Brouhard, R. (2019, April 29). How to Become a CPR Instructor. www.thebalancecareers.com/how-do-i-become-a-cpr-instructor-1298464

Bryson, M. (2018, January 26). How to Confidently Negotiate Your Rates as a Freelancer. millo.co/confidently-negotiate-rates-freelancer

Cattanach, J. (2019, August 12). How to Become a Freelance Writer: A Newbie's to Earn Money Writing. thewritelife.com/how-to-become-a-freelance-writer/

Cabler, J. (2013, June 3). Money Making Idea #3-Detailing Cars. www.cfinancialfreedom.com/money-making-idea-3-detailing-cars

Car Wash Business: Understanding the Pros and Cons. (2012, January 2). www.detailxperts.net/blog/2012/01/02/car-wash-business-understanding-the-pros-and-cons

Clark, M. (2020). 5 Biggest Challenges Of Being A Dog Walker. dogtime.com/lifestyle/21501-biggest-challenges-dog-walker

Cooper, P. (2019, August 8). How to Make Money on Youtube: 6 Effective strategies. blog.hootsuite.com/how-to-make-money-on-youtube/

Desmond, C. (2020). This Guy's Weekend Side Job Helps Him Earn Over 2K Each Summer. www.thepennyhoarder.com/make-money/side-gigs/summer-job-caddying/

Eden, A. (2019, April 2). Flea Market Flipping: Make Money Flipping Items For Profit. www.mintnotion.com/extra-income/flea-market-flipping-make-money-flipping-items-for-profit/

Edmonson, B. (2019, July 16). How to Start Affiliate Marketing. www.thebalancesmb.com/launching-affiliate-marketing-business-2531501

Elrick, L. (2017, September 19). Industry Experts Share the True Pros and Cons of Being a Graphic Designer. www.rasmussen.edu/degrees/design/blog/pros-and-cons-of-being-graphic-designer/

Ever, T. (2017, November 24). How to successfully Sell your Photos Online as a Photographer. graphpaperpress.com/blog/sell-photos-online/

Ferreira, N.M. (2020, March 12). 10 Best Side Hustle Ideas to Make an Extra $1,000 a Month. www.oberlo.com/blog/side-hustle

Foy, K. (2017, July 5). 7 Reasons Babysitting is the Perfect Side Hustle No Matter What Your Career is. hellogiggles.com/lifestyle/money-career/reasons-babysitting-is-the-perfect-side-hustle-no-matter-what-your-career-is/

Friedman, Z. (2020, February 3). *Student Loan Debt Statistics In 2020: A Record $1.6 Trillion*. Forbes. https://www.forbes.com/sites/zackfriedman/2020/02/03/student-loan-debt-statistics/#20979d01281f

Fuller, J. (2019, October 14). 7 Jobs at the Golf Course You Should Find Interesting. www.careermetis.com/golf-course-jobs-you-should-find-interesting/

Gojko, E. (2009, September 3). House Sitting for Your Neighbor: The Dos and Don'ts. ohmyapt.apartmentratings.com/house-sitting-for-your-neighbor-the-dos-and-donts.html

Hart, K. (2018). Why Caddying is a Great Job for High School Students. caddienow.com/why-caddying-is-a-great-job-for-high-school-students/

Hayes, J. (2020). Side Hustle Series No. 1-
Freelance Graphic Design.
www.jenhayes.me/side-hustle-series-no-1-
freelance-graphic-design

Hunt, M. (2017, September 11) 10 Money-Making
Side Hustles You Can Start for Free or
Cheaply.
www.entrepreneur.com/article/300024

Inetwork. (2018, July 27). 4 Fundamentals of Being
a Youths Sports Referee.
www.leaguenetwork.com/2018/07/4-
fundamentals-of-being-a-youth-sports-
referee/

Jobstreet.com. (2018, December 2). Freelancing
Tips for Beginners: Building Your Credibility
101.

Jorgovan, J. (2019, February 12). Pricing 101: How
to Price Yourself as a Freelancer.
http://careerfoundry.com/en/blog/career-
change/pricing-freelancer/

Kamariya, P. (2020). YouTube as a Career: Pros
and Cons. vidooly.com/blog/youtube-as-a-
career-pros-cons/

Kennedy, J. (2019, August 5). How to Become a
Successful Tutor.
www.care.com/c/stories/5383/how-to-
become-a-successful-tutor/

Knapp, J. (2019, December 16). How to Start a Blog-Beginners Guide for 2020. www.bloggingbasics101.com/how-do-i-start-a-blog

Marinov, V. (2019, March 21). 5 Must-Have Clauses for any Freelancer Contract. www.freelancermap.com/blog/5-must-have-clauses-for-any-freelancer-contract/

Music & Arts. (2018, April 26). How to Become a Private Music Teacher. http://thevault.musicarts.com/how-to-become-private-music-teacher/

Muller, C. (2020, May 12). How to Save Money as a Teen. https://www.moneyunder30.com/how-teens-can-save-money

Muller, C. (2020, May 25). 8 Ways to Get Your Teen to Start Investing. www.doughroller.net/investing/best-investments-for-teens/

Narumanchi, S. (2020, February 12). 8 Trusted Ways to Get House Sitting Jobs. crowdworknews.com/house-sitting-jobs/

Oberlo. (N.D.) What is Dropshipping? www.oberlo.com/ebooks/dropshipping/what-is-dropshipping

Philpott, L. (N.D.). Pros & Cons of Being a Dog Walker. www.petprofessional.com.au/info-centre/pros-cons-of-being-a-dog-walker

Ransbiz. (2017). 3 Disadvantages of Domain Flipping. www.ransbiz.com/2016/07/3-disadvantages-of-domain-flipping.html

Ransbiz. (2017). 7 Advantages of Flipping Domains as an Online Business. www.ransbiz.com/2016/06/7-advantages-of-flipping-domains-as.html

Schroeder-Garndner, M. (2018, May 30). 6 Actions to Take to Find Your First Customers When No one Knows You. www.makingsenseofcents.com/2018/05/how-to-find-customers-for-your-side-hustle.html

Saxena, P. 2020, May 20. How Much Money Can You Earn Through An App? Read Here. appinventiv.com/blog/how-much-money-can-you-earn-through-your-mobile-app/

Shain, S. (2019, September 23). Calling All Homemakers: Here's How to Earn Money Selling Your Treats. www.thepennyhoarder.com/make-money/side-gigs/selling-baked-goods-from-home/

Shoes For Crews Europe. (2020, May 19) The Honest Truth: What is it Like Working in a

Fast Food Restaurant.
blog.sfceurope.com/what-is-it-like-working-
in-a-fast-food-restaurant

SideHustleHQ. (2016). How To Start a Lawn Care
Business. sidehustlehq.com/how-to-start-a-
lawn-care-business/

SideHustleHQ. (2016). Making Money Buying and
Selling Domain Names.
sidehustlehq.com/making-money-buying-
and-selling-domain-names/

Slingerland, C. (2019, December 20). How to
Create an Ebook from Scratch in 2020.
moosend.com/blog/how-to-create-an-
eBook/

Suggett, P. (2019, November 29). Charging the Rate
You Deserve as a Freelancer.
www.thebalancecareers.com/freelancing-
charge-the-rate-you-deserve-38878

Torres, L. (2020). Retail Workers' Biggest
Challenges, Experts Advice From the Sales
Floor. www.monster.com/career-
advice/article/retail-workers-biggest-
challenges-and-expert-advice-from-the-
sales-floor

USA Today Classifieds. (N.D.). How To Work As A
Lifeguard On Your Summer Break.
classifieds.usatoday.com/blog/careers/work
-lifeguard-summer-break/

Vaynerchuk, G. (2019). 6 Garage Sale Flipping Strategies to Make Extra Money. www.garyvaynerchuk.com/garage-sale-flipping/

Varshneya, R. (2019 June 13). A Step-by-Step Guide to Building Your First Mobile App. www.entrepreneur.com/article/231145

Ward, S. (2019, June 25). 7 Ways to Make Sure You're Getting Paid By Customers and Clients. www.thebalancesmb.com/how-to-bill-a-customer-2948033

Winn, R. (2013, May 13). How to Start a Podcast: A Complete Step-by-Step Tutorial. www.podcastinsights.com/start-a-podcast/

Witmer, D. (2019, October 29). Teens and Income Tax. /www.thebalance.com/teens-and-income-taxes-2610240